FIVE
FORGOTTEN
TRUTHS

THE CHURCH MUST REMEMBER

JOHN R. GATERS

WESTBOW
PRESS®
A DIVISION OF THOMAS NELSON
& ZONDERVAN

WestBow Press books may be ordered through booksellers or by contacting:

WestBow Press
A Division of Thomas Nelson & Zondervan
1663 Liberty Drive
Bloomington, IN 47403
www.westbowpress.com
1 (866) 928-1240

ISBN: 978-1-5127-1714-3 (sc)
ISBN: 978-1-5127-1715-0 (hc)
ISBN: 978-1-5127-1713-6 (e)

Library of Congress Control Number: 2015917381

Print information available on the last page.

WestBow Press rev. date: 10/30/2015

This book is dedicated to my wife, Angela, without whom I never would have dared to try, and to our children, Paul, Mary Kate and Hannah, who grew up and became our friends. Thank you for your love.

Contents

INTRODUCTION -- THE NOTE-DROPPER

There was a particular Sunday morning that set me on a course of writing this book. It was a few years ago, and I was Minister of Music, Education, and Outreach at First Baptist Church. Our pastor had resigned to accept another position a couple of months earlier, and we did not have an interim, so each week we enjoyed a different visiting preacher. Well, we usually enjoyed them. A few were missionaries on furlough. Some were retired pastors gracious enough to come fill in for a church in need. A few were obviously interested in becoming our next pastor, and one or two, well, I wasn't sure about their motivation.

It was my responsibility to meet each visiting speaker, make sure he had whatever he needed, familiarize him with the wireless microphone, and help him feel welcome in our church. This particular Sunday morning I felt uneasy about our visitor. Some little red flags were going up in my spirit that made me think this guy was less than one hundred percent genuine, but I dutifully soldiered on. As our worship service began, I greeted the congregation with a smile, made the necessary announcements, and of course, gave our visitor the most gracious introduction possible under the circumstances. Some in our church noticed how uncomfortable I was that morning—transparency is something I had long prayed for—and rightly surmised that the guest speaker was the source of my discomfort.

When we reached the time for his sermon, the gentleman bounded onto the platform. He was full of energy and enthusiasm, and proceeded with a very shallow but exciting message. It was the standard, recognizable format you hear in most churches: a short passage of scripture, a brief prayer, followed by three points, more or less, and expanded with some funny stories or illustrations. Of course, there is normally an emotional poem to drive home the points made, or a story about someone who did not heed the warning of today's scripture passage and suffered the consequences. It was standard operating procedure, what most of us have become accustomed to.

Somehow, however, in the midst of point two or three—I forget which—our visiting preacher explained to us that he was anointed, and that an anointed preacher didn't have to use notes. He explained that he could simply step behind the pulpit and allow the Holy Spirit to speak through him. That, from his perspective, was the test of a true man of God. Just then, in his excitement, he jerked his bible from the pulpit, and several pieces of paper fell out, scattering all over the platform, a couple of them even landing at my feet, where I was seated on the front pew. The man was visibly and obviously embarrassed; his face blushed, and out of his mouth came these words: "Those aren't my notes!" I gazed down at one of the errant sheets of paper lying suspiciously at my feet. They were, in fact, sermon notes, quite detailed, even down to the invitation line, "every head bowed and every eye closed."

There was nervous laughter from the congregation, and I assumed that his cover was blown. I braced myself for an afternoon of questions and phone calls from church members wanting to know who was responsible for bringing in that guy. Fortunately for me, everyone knew it was not my job to fill the pulpit, so the reaction was fairly mild. "I wouldn't believe it if I hadn't seen it with my own eyes" was one man's comment. A lot of people present that morning, however, saw it and still didn't believe it. Some believed it but thought it wasn't important. In fact, I was shocked at how many phone calls I received from church members who wanted to make sure we had the man's resume. "He would make a great pastor!" some said to me.

Two things saddened me about that experience. First of all, it seemed tragic to me that a preacher would lie from the pulpit in an attempt to trick us into thinking he was an anointed man of God. Second, even more tragic was that half our congregation fell for it, in spite of the note-dropping incident.

You see, when people don't really know God's truths, they become gullible, and on that Sunday morning I realized just how gullible, and vulnerable, our sweet congregation had become. It wasn't just that incident on that Sunday morning that caused me to write this book. That morning was the beginning of an adventure that lasted another year and a half. It was exhausting, sometimes frightening, and always frustrating, but when it was over God had given me the title for this book. I knew there were certain truths about God that had been forgotten by the church, not just the congregation I served, but the church at large.

In the middle of that adventure, God also called me to become a pastor. My preaching and teaching ministry has been the research for this book. God has given me the opportunity to apply these truths to a congregation, and it has been a blessing. Thus, this book is written to the church. Yes, there is occasional criticism of things I see in the church that are wrong, but my motive in writing is not to criticize, but to encourage. These wrong things have often caused me pain and grief, and I suspect many of you would say the same. I have chosen to learn from these experiences, and to ask God to teach me the truths, the right things, so the wrong things can be corrected. My goal is that this book will strengthen your faith in God, help you feel loved by Him, and encourage you to share that with others. Ultimately, that will strengthen the church in America. With that said, there are five things, five truths, which I believe the church desperately needs to be reminded of.

Christians need to know and understand the truth of God's SOVEREIGNTY, the big picture, how he works, what he's doing in the world, and what our purpose is. Christians need to know and understand the truth about SALVATION, how sinners find God through Jesus Christ, how he pursues us, and what it means to be part of a covenant. Christians need to know and understand the truth about SANCTITY, how to be transformed and live a life of holiness and righteousness, how to stay in fellowship with God and communicate with him. Christians need to know and understand the truth about STEWARDSHIP, why we go to church, why we support it, and why we need to be involved in its work. Finally, Christians need to know and understand the truth about SHEPHERDS, the true ones and the fakes, how to know the difference, and the real responsibilities of our pastors and leaders.

AND WE KNOW THAT IN ALL THINGS GOD WORKS FOR THE GOOD OF THOSE WHO LOVE HIM, WHO HAVE BEEN CALLED ACCORDING TO HIS PURPOSE. ROMANS 8:28

PART ONE

THE
TRUTH
ABOUT
SOVEREIGNTY

CHAPTER ONE

THE BIG PICTURE

I grew up in church, and felt convicted to give my life to Christ when I was nine years old. Even though I didn't understand it at the time, it is obvious to me today that almost immediately I began to suspect there was more to Christianity than I was being taught. It was a good church, a sweet congregation, and certainly no one was trying to mislead me; not at all. It's just that, sitting in Sunday School and worship services week after week, being blessed and encouraged, and learning some fundamental truths, I still felt this strange feeling, as if we were missing something. It was like being lost in fog, where staying on the path was tricky, seeing ahead was impossible, looking around seemed pointless, all because of the murkiness of the fog. You cannot see the big picture when you're foggy, and certainly can't make sense of the details. This book is an effort to lift the fog that seems to surround the church today.

Well-meaning people over the years have reminded me of Psalm 119, verse 105, that beautifully states, *Your word is a lamp to my feet and a light for my path.* "John," they would say, "you're not supposed to see the big picture, just the next step on the path." Of course, I offered the obligatory nod of the head, as if I "got it," but the feeling of missing something didn't go away. You see, even that thoughtful explanation missed the mark, assuming that God intended for us to live at some level of ignorance. It limited God's ability, if you will, to teach us the big picture. It implied that the fog was intentional, and that living in faith meant accepting the fogginess.

That line of thought essentially says "you're not supposed to understand what God is doing, so stop trying!" That was unacceptable to me. Of course, there are some things we will probably never know this side of heaven, but it seemed odd to me, beyond logic, to think that this amazing God who loved me didn't want me to see or know what he was doing with us. "It's the Great Commission!" someone would say. "That's what it's all about!" Another person would say that it's all about personal growth, getting to be more like Jesus. As the years passed, however, I found myself twenty-six years old, still in the same church, still feeling a certain emptiness, still feeling engulfed in fog. You see, we seemed not to be very passionate about fulfilling the Great Commission or becoming more Christ-like. We said all the right things and knew all the right answers, but we weren't asking the right questions. We were missing the mark, but didn't even know it. I sensed it, but didn't know where the "mark" was. Today I know that we were missing the **truth about sovereignty**.

Term to Remember: SOVEREIGNTY means "supreme authority." When someone is sovereign he has all the authority and power. God is sovereign over the entire universe. The Bible teaches that God is the supreme Ruler and Lawgiver.

My father is a builder, and when I was a kid I often went to work with him over summer break. He could drive a nail like nobody else. In fact, he could hold a nail, a big one, and tap it once to "set it." Then he would draw back his hammer, and in one powerful swing, drive that nail completely into the wood. He could do that every time, all day long. He could hit the nail on the head, literally, because he could see it. At church, however, we seemed more like children at a birthday party, playing pin-the-tail-on-the-donkey, or swinging wildly at a piñata, always blindfolded. That's funny to watch when you're playing games, but tragic when you're playing with people's souls. That's the problem with the fog—it acts as a blindfold.

The nail, of course, does not represent the big picture in this feeble analogy. The big picture would be the house under construction. The problem with building a house is in knowing how it all goes together.

There are thousands of pieces of wood, metal, plastic, nails, screws, etc. that eventually make a complete house—a big picture. But to be a successful builder, you must know the parts. In other words, "why **this** nail," and "why **here**?" What purpose does it serve?

THE GENERAL REVELATION

At this point, you may be thinking, "Okay, I get the analogy, but what exactly are we talking about here?" If it seems fuzzy to you, hold on and keep reading. We have to look at the parts first as a whole. What I mean is, we're going to look at the house first and get a feel for the layout. You might say we're doing a home inspection, to see how this "big picture" is put together. Then we can start examining the individual parts of the structure. When we're done, I pray that you will see it with new eyes— that you will marvel at the magnificent structure in a way you've never marveled before. More importantly, I pray that you will be awestruck by the builder, God Almighty.

The big picture--we are going to look at it as a house, a very large and beautiful house. It's not that this house is the biggest or the best house on the street; it's the ONLY house on the street. In fact, it's the only house PERIOD. There are no other houses. There are no other builders. One Builder. One house.

Point: The Bible teaches that there is only one true God. His creation confirms it.

However, this house was built to impress you. Psalm 19:1 says *the heavens declare the glory of God; the skies proclaim the work of his hands.* You see, God created the universe on such a magnificent scale so we would take notice of it and be impressed by it. That way, we would know that the one who created it all is great and worthy of our attention. In other words, he wanted us to know that he is God—that he is divine, not imperfect like us, but perfect. He also wanted us to see that he is not natural, like us. He is supernatural. He has always existed and always will. He is eternal. Romans 1:20 tells us, *For since the creation of the world God's invisible qualities--his eternal power and divine nature-- have been clearly seen, being understood from what has been made, so that men are without excuse.* So when you explore God's creation, the house, you are amazed at its size. It has more rooms than you can count. The materials it is made of are exquisite. The craftsmanship of its construction is so precise, so orderly, and so well thought-out. It is simply too enormous for you to explore it all or understand how it was built. But make no mistake, it was designed and built out of love to impress you, to make you notice God. He wants your attention!

This is what scholars call the General Revelation. It means that God has revealed himself to us in a general way by showing us his creative power. *So that men are without excuse* simply means that no one will ever be able to stand before God at the end, and say, "Gee, I didn't know you were real!" Don't overlook this important first point. Atheists are not ignorant. They know God is real. They choose to deny the truth. Let's take a closer look at this general revelation, or what God has **generally revealed** to all of humanity.

Term to Remember: GENERAL REVELATION means that the universe that God created shows us some general truths about him. These truths are revealed to us by what we can see.

Let's look again at Romans 1:20 but add in verses 18 and 19. *The wrath of God is being revealed from heaven against all the godlessness and wickedness of men who suppress the truth by their wickedness, since what may be known about God is plain to them, because God has made it plain to them. For since the creation of the world God's invisible qualities--his eternal power and divine nature—have been clearly seen, being understood from what has been made, so that men are without excuse.*

Let's go back to our analogy. The big picture is the house God built—the universe and all it contains. He is telling us in Romans 1 that his fingerprints are all over that house. What he built looks like something only he would build. It tells us three important things about him. 1) He exists! The house didn't just magically appear. Someone built it. There is a

Builder. 2) His power is eternal. He has always existed. He wasn't born, or created by some other life form. He didn't start out human and evolve into a supremely powerful God. He always has been what He is now. 3) He is divine. He is holy and righteous. There is nothing bad or evil or imperfect about Him. These are the things He wants every single human being to know about him, even if they never set foot inside a church building. Even if they never hear the gospel message of Jesus Christ, there are certain things they know about God because of what he has built. This is a very important point to remember.

Point: ETERNAL means God has always existed. He was here before anything else. ETERNAL POWER means he is the source of all power. He didn't *become* powerful. He always was and always will be all-powerful. DIVINE means "holy." DIVINE NATURE means that God didn't *decide* to be holy—holiness comes naturally to him. It's part of his nature. He can't be anything other than holy.

Several years ago I built a house for my family. It isn't elaborate or grand, but it is unique. There is a lot of reclaimed wood inside my house, which, by the way, required a great deal of labor to reclaim! The house has lots of character, lots of things only my feeble mind would dream up for a house. I built it for my family. I built it with love, and it definitely carries my fingerprints, literally and figuratively. In fact, when people visit, they often say, "John, this house looks like something you would build!" Even someone who had never met me and knew nothing about me could draw certain conclusions about me if they walked around my house. For example, they would rightly assume that my taste is pretty traditional, and that I like historical style, since my home is based on an early 19th century design. The observer might conclude that I'm not lazy, since there are quite a few design elements that were obviously labor-intensive, and they might also think I have great patience. When they saw the room I fixed for my wife's crafting projects, they might also conclude, rightly so, that I'm a doting husband. In fact, these are all things people have said when touring our house, and yes, it makes me smile proudly when I hear it.

Now consider what God said after he completed his creative work: *God saw all that he had made, and it was very good,* Genesis 1:31. God smiled proudly, because what he had made reflected his character. Just as my home reflects who I am and how I live, God's incredible universe reflects who he is, and how we should live. He has used what he made to supernaturally convict us of his presence, his eternal power, and his divine nature. His handiwork says something about him and his nature. He did that out of love. He wants you to seek him out. He wants you to know the truth about him.

But understand this: God becomes very angry at those who *suppress the truth* about him. This general revelation is the first step in knowing God, and Satan uses people, who choose not to believe, to try and sway others into unbelief. God plainly states at the end of Romans 1:20 that *men are without excuse.* So, as I mentioned earlier, no one will ever stand before God and claim they didn't know he was real. No one. Now let's take it a little further.

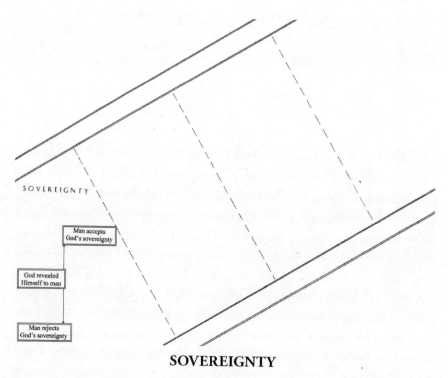

SOVEREIGNTY

MORE SPECIFICALLY

Some people think we live our lives just wandering aimlessly through this house we keep talking about, but that's not really accurate. God has been leading mankind through the house, putting different cultures and civilizations in the right room at the right time. The apostle Paul tried to explain this to the people of Athens. Acts 17:26-28 records his words: *from one man he made every nation of men, that they should inhabit the whole earth; and he determined the times set for them and the exact places where they should live. God did this so that men would seek him and perhaps reach out for him, though he is not far from each one of us. For in him we live and move and have our being.*

God has been actively involved in human history. He didn't just create us; put us in this house and say, "Good luck!" He created a house majestic enough to let us know he is there, the great eternal, divine builder. He also hopes it will intrigue us and make us want to know more about him, to seek him, and he has been leading humans from the beginning to prod us along in our looking. Have you ever wondered why humans are so curious? God made us that way, wanting us to be curious about him, to look for him. He wants to be found! He wants us to know the truth about his sovereignty.

Point: God is personal. He wants a relationship with you. That truth makes Christianity different from most religions—they often teach that God is supreme and powerful but out of reach. Christianity is unique in teaching that you can have a personal relationship with God.

It gets even more interesting, however, when you consider the teaching of Jesus found in Matthew 5:45, *He causes the sun to rise on the evil and the good, and sends rain on the righteous and the unrighteous.* God has placed a blanket of love over all his creation, even the ones who reject him, in the hope that they will seek him out. In the verse just before that, Jesus said, *love your enemies and pray for those who persecute you.* So yes, God does become angry with those who try to suppress the truth about him, but our God loves all of us enough to share some of his love even with those who don't really want it, and commands Christians to love them as well. Now that is love! It must be easy for God to love those who praise him, but he also loves those who don't. The sun and the rain are just two more examples of how God's love motif is carved into every nook and cranny of this great house. They also are an example of his sovereignty. He reigns over each and every one of us, whether or not we believe it or accept it.

So, God made sure we would know he is there, and has hoped we would seek him. He has even orchestrated human history to help us in our searching. However, God has gone much further than that. He has done some really big things to teach us more about him, to make us even more curious. He has revealed himself to us. Scholars call it Dispensationalism, but it's basically just the concept of God telling us more and more about himself as history unfolds.

Term to Remember: DISPENSATION means that God had a plan for dispensing, or revealing, information about himself to humans.

Some scholars only recognize two dispensations—the old and new covenants. Others recognize three or four. I, and many other evangelicals, prefer the breakdown of God's revelation to us into seven dispensations. The most important point is that God has revealed himself to humanity. How we break that down isn't critical. Hopefully, however, this method of interpreting scripture will help you see, better than ever, how much effort God has made to show us who he is.

Let's start at our beginning. God created the heavens and the earth as part of his plan of redemption. Yes, God had a plan all along, and that plan included creation. This is important, because many people wrongly teach that God's plan of redemption was reactionary—that God created, man sinned, and God came up with a plan to deal with it. The scripture tells us in Revelation 13:8 that Jesus is the *"Lamb that was slain from the creation of the world."* God created everything, including humans, knowing we would require redemption. God did not simply react to sin—he created with the intention of dealing with sin and evil once and for all. That's why it is so important for us to know the truth about God and his sovereignty. That's why it is so important for us to seek God. That's why he created on such a magnificent scale, and it was all part of this great master plan, the plan of redemption. (That's the big picture we're calling a house) He created Adam and Eve and put them in the middle of it all. Now, they knew God personally and had fellowship with him, so that wasn't the problem. The problem was, they disobeyed him. You see, God only gave them one rule—don't eat the fruit from the tree of the knowledge of good and evil. He told them that if they did eat from it they would die. This was the first dispensation, or what humans knew about God beyond the general revelation, and it's often called the dispensation of **Innocence**.

Term to Remember: INNOCENCE means that Adam and Eve were capable of sinning, but at that point never had. They were literally innocent.

Adam and Eve were innocent. They had never experienced evil, though they were apparently aware of its existence. God had not formally told them very much about himself, but there was no need to. They knew he was the builder/creator, and the one who builds the house and owns it gets to make the rules, and he only gave them one rule to obey. They knew everything they needed to know in order to live in a peaceful, happy relationship with God, but they broke the one rule.

The Lord God took the man and put him in the Garden of Eden to work it and take care of it. And the Lord God commanded the man, "you are free to eat from any tree in the garden; but you must not eat from the tree of the knowledge of good and evil, for when you eat of it you will surely die." Genesis 2:15-17. Adam and Eve were literally, and totally, innocent up to this point. Theologians love to debate whether or not the fruit itself had any significance. Did ingesting that particular fruit actually expand their knowledge of good and evil? Or was it their disobedience that opened their eyes? It is not relevant to my point. The fruit was a test of obedience. All that God required of them to maintain their perfect fellowship with him was to obey his one simple rule—*do not eat from the tree.*

Adam, of course, had the general revelation of God that is evident in creation, but he also enjoyed, along with his wife, a close and personal relationship with God. In the verses above, God spoke directly to Adam. We learn from Genesis 3 that God was present in the garden with them. This is an interesting point to consider—in God's original set-up, he and man were in perfect fellowship. Remember, this is how God established his relationship with humans. The distance we sometimes feel, the fogginess we navigate through—none of that was God's doing. It was man's sin that created the fog.

Point: If your relationship with God seems distant or strained, that is not how he wants it. That is not how he planned it. Remember, he is a personal God. He wants to be known.

Think about it. If we go back to the analogy, God built this magnificent house, designed to impress Adam. Adam was free to run around in the house and enjoy its comforts, its beauty, but even better, God himself joined him, walking and fellowshipping with him in the garden. And there was only one rule to live by. It's as if God said, "You two can have the run of the house. Just stay out of the closet in the second floor hallway." But of course, Satan came along and said, "You guys just HAVE to see what's in that closet!" So they disobeyed God. They were no longer innocent. They had experienced evil. They had broken their perfect fellowship with God. That leads us to the second dispensation, often called **Moral Responsibility.**

Term to Remember: MORAL RESPONSIBILITY means that once Adam and Eve had experienced evil, they were no longer innocent. They now had to make a moral choice to serve God or reject him.

Once their innocence was lost, Adam and Eve had a responsibility. They learned from their experience that God, the builder of the house, has an enemy, Satan. Satan is not a builder. He is a destroyer. God demands an orderly house, but Satan tries to bring chaos and confusion into the house. He is the one who pushed Adam and Eve to disobey God in the first place, and now some of the order was gone. That disobedience was sin, and sin has certain serious affects on humans. When Adam and Eve disobeyed God and sinned, they died spiritually—their perfect fellowship with God was broken. Sin interferes with our sensory understanding of God. 1 Corinthians 13 teaches about gaining spiritual maturity, but verse 12 acknowledges that even the mature *see but a poor reflection as in a mirror; then we shall see face to face.* It is important to remember that God created us knowing we would sin and lose some of our sight. That's where the general revelation comes into play. God planned creation so that, even in a sinful state, with poor vision, we would see evidence of him and know he is there. He created on such a grand scale because he knew that sin would interfere with us when we looked for him.

So spiritual death was the first effect of sin on humanity, and God had already made arrangements to deal with that problem for us. The plan of redemption was in place before we were created. Also, the long-term effects of sin caused their bodies to wear out and die. That's physical death. Neither type of death, spiritual nor physical, was part of God's plan. Satan introduced death to mankind, but now it is here, and humans have to take responsibility for their actions. Thus we have the dispensation of Moral Responsibility.

Now, every person born on this earth has to take responsibility for his sin. Adam and Eve had children, and two of their sons show us the difference between taking responsibility and not. Abel gave sacrifices to God and worshiped him, the builder. He made the choice to serve the builder (God) and not the destroyer (Satan). The proof wasn't in his actions but in his heart, and only God can really see that deep, because Cain, Abel's brother, made sacrifices and went through the motions of worship, but it wasn't genuine. Genesis 4:4-5 says *The Lord looked with favor on Abel and his offering, but on Cain and his offering he did not look with favor. So Cain was very angry, and his face was downcast.* God approved of Abel's effort because of the motive behind it. Abel wanted to please God and be submissive to him. He recognized that God was the builder and owner of the house (the General Revelation), and he knew he was not innocent (1ˢᵗ Dispensation). He also wanted to accept responsibility for his sinful nature (2ⁿᵈ Dispensation) by choosing to serve God.

What Cain and Abel both knew about God:
General Revelation > Innocence > Moral Responsibility

In other words, Abel recognized the sovereignty of God, and was very humble before him. Cain, on the other hand, just wanted to appease God. Here's the proof: when God told him his motives weren't right, Cain didn't humble himself and repent. He just got angry. In verse 7 of Genesis 4, God told him *If you do what is right, will you not be accepted? But if you do not do what is right, sin is crouching at your door; it desires to have you, but you must master it.* God was telling Cain that he had a choice to make, a moral responsibility, to choose good or evil, God or Satan. Guess which choice Cain made? He got so angry with God that he went and murdered his brother. Notice I did not say that Cain was angry with his brother, but with God. After all, it was God who confronted his attitude. It was God who let him know he was falling short of expectations. It was Abel, however, who suffered Cain's wrath.

Question: Why do bad things happen to good people? It's a question as old as human history. God created us with freedom of choice. Without it, we wouldn't be free to sin, like Cain did, and hurt other people. But, we wouldn't be free to choose to do the right thing either. We wouldn't be free to choose to love God and place our faith in him. We could serve him like robots, but he prefers a more personal relationship—one of mutual love. That type of relationship requires freedom and with freedom comes responsibility.

This is the root of modern unbelief, or atheism. It's not that some people just cannot accept the possibility of God—they don't want there to be a God. If God is real, then he is sovereign! He has to be! Many people choose not to believe rather than think themselves accountable to a sovereign Creator. I hear atheists shout "there is no God!" and in the next sentence explain to us how horrible they think he is. By insulting God, they are accepting the premise that he exists, and don't even realize it. For Cain, however, God was apparently talking directly to him, so he could not ignore the reality of God, but he sure did get angry at being held accountable. Instead of mastering sin, sin had mastered him.

That's pretty much the choice most people made, and the world became so wicked that God chose to destroy just about everything with a global flood. He saved Noah, and his family, because Noah was a righteous man who served God. After the flood, when Noah and his family got off the ark, God shared a little more information about himself. This is the third dispensation, often called **Human Government.**

Term to Remember: HUMAN GOVERNMENT means that God gave humans some civil laws to go by. It was intended to make it easier for them to govern themselves by setting some standards. It also emphasized the value of human life.

God made it known to Noah that he loves humans and values human life. So, you ask, why did God destroy most of them if He loved them? Good question. Remember, God built the house and desires order and peace, but Satan introduced rebellion, disorder, and violence. Satan introduced death. God is determined to make it right again, to redeem mankind. He's not going to allow anyone, Satan or any human, to stop his plan of redemption. A loving God will protect his plan of redemption and do whatever is necessary to make redemption available. Satan's plan has always been to turn people away from God, to thwart God's plan, to keep redemption out of this world. It is likely that Satan knew God would send his Son to save us, and he worked very hard in Noah's day to try and prevent that from happening.

God took drastic measures to keep the plan on track. Genesis 6:11 says *Now the earth was corrupt in God's sight and was full of violence.* Cain's violent attitude toward God had spread over the entire population. Also, keep in mind that the people living before the flood knew God was there, that he is divine and eternal (the general revelation). They also knew their fellowship with him was broken and they were not innocent any longer (1st dispensation-innocence). Plus, they knew, like Cain did, that they had a moral responsibility (2nd dispensation) to either serve God or serve Satan.

Question: Did the people who died in the flood deserve punishment? Many say "No, that's not fair!" But what did these people know about God and what did they do to deserve punishment? They knew what Abel knew and he made the right choice. They did not. They rejected God's sovereignty. They went the way of Cain. Remember what they knew about God:

General Revelation > Innocence > Moral Responsibility

Also, 2 Peter 2:5 describes Noah as a *preacher of righteousness.* There is certainly every reason to believe that many people witnessed Noah's ark-building project. It would have been quite a spectacle, and since it took quite a long time, many may have traveled to see it. It is conjecture, I know, but if we take the scripture literally, then Noah, either by his actions, his words, or both, was preaching righteousness to a very unrighteous population. These were not innocent, ignorant people who were executed by an angry, out-of-control God. These were people who knew who he was but chose to rebel against him. They were helping Satan ransack the house and God stopped it. A loving God was obligated to stop it. More about that later.

That's why he set up some boundaries after the flood. (3rd dispensation--Human Government) God told Noah that from now on, anyone who committed murder would be accountable to the rest of society. Genesis 9:5 says *And from each man, too, I will demand an accounting for the life of his fellow man. Whoever sheds the blood of man, by man shall his blood be shed, for in the image of God has God made man.* Before the flood, humans weren't taking God's love for humanity very seriously. As we noted in the previous paragraph, God was very unhappy that his earth was full of violence, so after the flood he let it be known that he wouldn't tolerate their callous attitude toward human life. God instituted human government to set up some boundaries and make us accountable to each other to protect life. God wants peace and order in his house, and he can't fellowship with us when we are in chaos and disorder. That's the important thing to remember here: God wants a relationship with you!

Question: Is capital punishment fair? The death penalty, as enacted by God, was designed to protect humans from each other. It showed how much God values human life and how far he would go to protect it. When humans reduce the punishment for murder they actually devalue human life, contrary to God's desires.

This third dispensation, human government, is a brilliant litmus test for humanity. God made it clear that he loves all the residents of his house and values their lives, so how well we value their lives shows how much we really value and love the Master of the house. 1 John 4:19-21 explains it so well: *We love because he first loved us. If anyone says, "I love God," yet hates his brother, he is a liar. For anyone who does not love his brother, whom he has seen, cannot love God, whom he has not seen. And he has given us this command: Whoever loves God must also love his brother.*

Each dispensation builds on the one before, and each one builds on the general revelation. So let's review. If you know God is there, that he is eternal and divine, that he makes the rules, and you choose to serve and worship him, then that love will show in the way you love his other children. Maybe you thought all the love talk started in the New Testament, but God's plan has had love printed all over it from the very beginning. If there is one major design element in this great house God has built, it is love. It's like a motif; carved in the mantelpiece, etched in the window glass, printed on the wallpaper, woven into the rugs.....you get the idea. It is a house of love. God loves you!

CHAPTER TWO

THE FOCUS NARROWS

There's a fourth dispensation, often called the **Promise**, but it wasn't given to all the residents in the house, just a few that God chose for a special purpose. Let me explain why God did it this way. Up to this point, God has been revealing more and more information about himself, but humans haven't been listening very well. There are some righteous people who love and honor God, but most are just doing their own thing, living to satisfy their own desires. Again, it was Paul who explained it best in Romans 1:20-23, *For since the creation of the world God's invisible qualities--his eternal power and divine nature--have been clearly seen, being understood from what has been made, so that men are without excuse. For although they knew God, they neither glorified him as God nor gave thanks to him, but their thinking became futile and their foolish hearts were darkened. Although they claimed to be wise, they became fools, and exchanged the glory of the immortal God for images made to look like mortal men and birds and animals and reptiles.*

Term to Remember: PROMISE means that God promised he would send the world a Savior. He first made this promise to Abraham.

God made a big effort to make sure we know he is here, but most humans just thumbed their noses at him and worshiped something else. As an aside, isn't it interesting that people everywhere throughout all of history want to worship *something*? It is, I believe, the result of this general revelation, this knowledge of God's existence implanted in our conscience. God made us to want to worship, to desire a relationship with someone greater than us. It's because he wants us to know he is there, but unfortunately, many deny the truth inside them and seek to worship something other than the Master of the house. So, God, who is very patient and kind, determined, as part of his plan of redemption, to *show* us how we should relate to him.

Question: Why do the Jewish people even exist? They are called "God's chosen people" because their purpose was to live as an example to the world. This is also why they have always been hated by those who rebel against God's sovereignty.

He called out a man named Abram, changed his name to Abraham, promised him a lot of descendants, promised to make them into a great nation, and promised to bless the whole world through them. Genesis 12:1-3 records the promise God made to Abraham and his descendants: *The Lord had said to Abram, "Leave your country, your people and your father's household and go to the land I will show you. I will make you into a great nation and I will bless you; I will make your name great, and you will be a blessing. I will bless those who bless you, and whoever curses you I will curse; and all peoples on earth will be blessed through you."* These are the Jewish people who became the nation of Israel, and the promise was for a Redeemer, Jesus Christ. Galatians 3:16 teaches us about this promise when it says, *The promises were spoken to Abraham and to his seed. The Scripture does not say "and to seeds," meaning many people, but "and to your seed," meaning one person, who is Christ.* Paul, the author of Galatians, is referring to Genesis 22:18, where God restated his promise to Abraham: *And through your offspring* (seed) *all nations on earth will be blessed, because you have obeyed me.*

Let's go back to our analogy. God made this great big, incredible house and filled it with people. He gave everybody the same information, kind of like posting it on the refrigerator door or the family bulletin board.

The problem is that very few are really getting the message. They all have access to it—they just aren't that interested in what God has to say, so God offers another approach. He chooses a small group, the Jews, and gives them more information about himself and his plan, the big picture, the house. He does this so the rest of the world, or residents, could watch his relationship with this group and realize what they are missing. Since humans had not listened very well with their ears, he gave them a chance to see with their eyes. He was showing the world the kind of close, loving relationship they could have with him.

Perhaps King Solomon of Israel understood better than anyone Israel's role in the world. He knew that when his nation served God faithfully, they would experience God's blessing, but if they turned from him, they would suffer discipline. After he built the great temple in Jerusalem, Solomon offered a prayer of dedication, recorded in 1 Kings 8. Part of the king's prayer was this: *When the heavens are shut up and there is no rain because your people have sinned against you, and when they pray toward this place and confess your name and turn from their sin because you have afflicted them, then hear from heaven and forgive the sin of your servants, your people Israel. Teach them the right way to live, and send rain on the land you gave your people for an inheritance.*

Solomon understood that God had set them apart, chosen them, to be an example of righteous living, serving and loving God, and their fortune or misfortune would be a direct result of how well they obeyed him. Solomon also realized why God did this. He knew the other nations would be watching and observing. He knew they would be comparing their false gods with Israel's true God. Remember, the world hasn't been listening to God very well, so he gives them an opportunity to see him at work. Solomon realized that their role on earth was evangelism! At one point in his dedication prayer, he said *as for the foreigner who does not belong to your people Israel but has come from a distant land because of your name—for men will hear of your great name and your mighty hand and your outstretched arm—when he comes and prays toward this temple, then hear from heaven, your dwelling place, and do whatever the foreigner asks of you, so that all the peoples of the earth may know your name and fear you, as do your own people Israel, and may know that this house I have built bears your name. 1 Kings 8:41-43*

Let me paraphrase. Solomon was saying that people would watch Israel and realize that God is there, that he is great and mighty, the One True God, and that he wants a relationship with them, and some of them would travel to the temple in Jerusalem seeking him. He asked God to answer their prayers so they would go back home telling everyone about the True God of Israel. The Jewish people were called to evangelize the nations—to teach them who God is. That is why God chose them, set them apart, and promised to bless the whole world through them. However, as mentioned earlier, God gave this chosen people more information about himself and his plan. He promised to send a Redeemer, through them, to the world.

GOD PROTECTS HIS PROMISE

A few pages back I talked about God using the flood to keep his plan of redemption on track. Satan tried to so corrupt the human race that God couldn't possibly send Jesus to take on human form. God took drastic measures. This is very important to understand, because scoffers tell us that the God of the Old Testament is a wrathful and angry God. Atheists in particular like to talk about God's anger and wrath. I don't have a problem with either! Let me explain why.

Satan did not give up after the flood and stop attacking God's plan. He used other people groups to oppress and attack the Jewish people, because Jesus Christ was promised to come into the world as a Jew. I'm not sure if Satan thought he could eradicate the Jewish people, but he certainly tried! And he has tried many times since, even in the 20th century. He will try again. Satan hates Israel because God used them to bring Jesus into the world, but God has protected them and kept them from being wiped off the earth. God sometimes called the Jewish people to war, because there were other people groups, prompted by Satan, who were bent on destroying, attacking, or otherwise harassing them. Here's one example:

When the Jewish people were traveling through the desert, they asked permission to pass peacefully through the country of the Amorites. They promised to stay on the highway, and not to consume water or vegetation. They simply wanted to pass through. Numbers 21:23-24 records the results. *But Sihon* (king of the Amorites) *would not let Israel pass through his territory. He mustered his entire army and marched out into the desert against Israel. When he reached Jahaz, he fought with Israel. Israel, however, put him to the sword and took over his land from the Arnon to the Jabbok, but only as far as the Ammonites, because their border was fortified.*

Another people group, the Moabites, witnessed this and were terrified of the Jews, even though God had made it clear to Moses that the Moabites were not their enemy. *Then the Lord said to me, "Do not harass the Moabites or provoke them to war, for I will not give you any part of their land. I have given Ar to the descendants of Lot as a possession"* Deuteronomy 2:9. The Moabites were descendants of Lot, Abraham's nephew. These were not ignorant people who knew nothing about God or his chosen people. They would have known all about Abraham and God's calling on his life and his descendants. They could have welcomed the Jewish people to the area, but instead they teamed up with the Midianites, and even hired a prophet, Balaam, to curse the Jews. But, God didn't allow Balaam to curse his people.

Eventually, Israel's enemies determined that the only way to destroy them was to weaken them, and the only way to weaken them was to come between them and their God. Yes, the Moabites and the Midianites recognized that the God of Israel was a great and powerful God—**they just didn't want to have anything to do with him**! You must understand this critical point. They didn't want to have peace with God or his people. They wanted to destroy God's people. They did not accept God's sovereignty. In fact, it was God who stood in the way of their plans. The Moabites and Midianites knew that Israel could be defeated if Israel betrayed their powerful sovereign God.

So they launched a plan. Their women enticed the Jewish men sexually, and *invited them to the sacrifices to their gods. The people ate and bowed down before these gods. So Israel joined in worshiping the Baal of Peor. And the Lord's anger burned against them,* Numbers 25:2-3. God ordered Moses to kill the leaders of these people, and told Israel's judges *to put to death those of your young men who have joined in worshiping the Baal of Peor.* verse 5. Furthermore, God told Moses in verses 17-18, *"treat the Midianites as enemies and kill them, because they treated you as enemies when they deceived you in the affair of Peor…"*

We already discussed the fact that God gets angry with those who suppress the truth about him, and the Moabites and Midianites were perfect examples of people who almost certainly knew the truth about God but worked very hard to suppress it, because they worshiped creatures rather than the Creator. By making themselves enemies of God's chosen evangelists, they made themselves enemies of God Almighty. That never works out. God had a plan of redemption in place, a plan that included the nation of Israel. It was a loving plan, a plan to offer salvation to all the world, and a loving God would never allow anyone to stop that plan. Anyone who tried faced his anger and wrath, including the Jewish people who fell into the deception.

Think of it this way. What if I was sitting in my home one night with my family and an intruder suddenly began beating down my front door, and I did nothing to stop him? What if the intruder broke into my home and began assaulting my wife and children, and I did nothing to stop him? Suppose he killed my family, and I just sat there? Would you call me a hero? Not likely. You might call me a wimp, a coward, or an idiot, but you wouldn't call me a hero. Some would even suggest that I be charged with involuntary manslaughter, since I did nothing to defend my home or family. I would be considered a fool. No one would respect me. However, if I retrieved my pistol and defended my family, I would be called a hero for saving four lives! Even if I killed the intruder, it would be considered self-defense, and I would still be a hero. So why then, do some argue that God is wrong for getting angry or showing His wrath when people attack his plan, or attack his chosen ones, or attack him? Why would we want to worship a God who doesn't defend what he loves? Quite frankly, I would be uncomfortable with God if that were his character. I find great comfort in a God who is unashamedly sovereign and unapologetically in control!

- -

Point: When something bad happens to me, I can rest assured that God has allowed it. If he allowed it, then it is not something that would destroy me or stop God's plan for my life. In fact, if God allows it then he can use it.

- -

Let's review for a moment. God built this great house and filled it with people. He made sure we knew he was there, eternal and divine. When we sinned, he showed us we were not innocent any longer. He told us to choose between him and his enemy. He told us to value human life the way he does, and made us accountable to one another for it. As I said before, he posted all this on the refrigerator door, carved his love into every nook and cranny, but most residents of the house still chose to act as if they owned the house themselves. They denied the truth of God's sovereignty. So he took a different and drastic approach. He pulled aside a small group in the house, the Jews, and dealt with them more directly. He made them an example for everyone else. He defended his plan. He protected the people through whom Jesus Christ would come; making certain redemption would be available for the world. God is a hero!

Point: God is a hero. He has a plan to save people. He protected that plan so that Satan couldn't steal it from you.

As an aside, I cannot understand people today who are bitter towards God, thinking he has somehow not done enough; blaming him for the chaos in the house; thinking he should **do something!** Hopefully, it is obvious to you by now that God loves us very much, that he craves a relationship with us, and that he has gone to great lengths to show us how to find him. He has exercised tremendous patience on our behalf, and has worked hard to keep the plan on track. This might be a good time to pause and thank him.

There is a fifth dispensation, also given exclusively to the Jewish people, and it is called the **Law.** Although this law encompassed every aspect of Jewish life, how they should live their lives to honor God, the most basic principles are what we know as the Ten Commandments. They are listed in Exodus 20, verses 3-17:

1. *You shall have no other gods before me.*
2. *You shall not make for yourselves an idol in the form of anything in heaven above or on the earth beneath or in the waters below. You shall*

not bow down to them or worship them; for I, the Lord your God,
am a jealous God, punishing the children for the sin of the fathers to
the third and fourth generation of those who hate me, but showing
love to a thousand generations of those who love me and keep my
commandments.

3. You shall not misuse the name of the Lord your God, for the Lord will
not hold anyone guiltless who misuses his name.

4. Remember the Sabbath day by keeping it holy. Six days you shall labor
and do all your work, but the seventh day is a Sabbath to the Lord
your God. On it you shall not do any work, neither you, nor your son
or daughter, nor your manservant or maidservant, nor your animals,
nor the alien within your gates. For in six days the Lord made the
heavens and the earth, the sea, and all that is in them, but he rested
on the seventh day. Therefore the Lord blessed the Sabbath day and
made it holy.

5. Honor your father and your mother, so that you may live long in the
land the Lord your God is giving you.

6. You shall not murder.

7. You shall not commit adultery.

8. You shall not steal.

9. You shall not give false testimony against your neighbor.

10. You shall not covet your neighbor's house. You shall not covet your
neighbor's wife, or his manservant or maidservant, his ox or donkey,
or anything that belongs to your neighbor.

Term to Remember: THE LAW means that God gave us, through
the Jewish people, a written account of his standards. It tells us what
God expects of us and shows us how we fall short.

Keep in mind, of all the residents living in the house, only the Jews are
given this law. It's not that God didn't care how the rest of the population
lived—He cared a lot, so much so that he called the Jewish people to be
an example of how to live. Also, most humans at this point had not obeyed
the basic house rules set up by God, the Master of the house, so it would

seem pointless to give them more rules and detailed laws to live by. God called Israel to be part of his plan of redemption by displaying a proper relationship with him. The responsibility to live up to these new rules fell on God's chosen evangelists, the Jewish people.

Point: Salvation is a gift from God, but it comes with responsibility. We must live as an example for others who have not yet accepted the gift.

So, what was the reason for this new law? Well, for starters, it gave the Jews more information about God and his character. It is always good to know more about someone who desires a relationship with you. But the law also was meant to prepare them for the promised coming Redeemer. Paul explained it in Galatians 3:19, *What, then, was the purpose of the law? It was added because of transgressions until the Seed (Redeemer) to whom the promise referred had come.* In other words, the law made sin more personal. The law proved that humans weren't simply guilty in the collective sense, but that each individual human was guilty of not meeting God's standards. Paul also wrote about this in Romans 3:20, *Therefore no one will be declared righteous in his sight by observing the law; rather, through the law we become conscious of sin.* You've no doubt heard the line, "The first step in getting help is admitting you have a problem!"

That was God's intention by giving the Jewish people a written copy of his rules, his standards. You need to know you have a sin problem if you're going to recognize that you need to be saved from that sin problem. You need to know the standard if you're going to recognize that you're missing it. You need to know how you're NOT living up to the standard to recognize that you need someone to help you. Better still, God sent Someone to live up to the standard for you. That's what Jesus meant when he said of God's laws, *I have not come to abolish them but to fulfill them.* He came to do for us what we could not accomplish on our own. Romans 3:22-23 tells us that *righteousness comes from God through faith in Jesus Christ to all who believe. There is no difference, for all have sinned and fall short of the glory of God...* So here's the big point about the law: it was always meant to make us WANT a Savior, and God had every intention of providing us One. God, through the Law, and through His chosen people, was preparing an unrighteous world for righteousness.

THE LAW—Why I need a Savior
PROMISE—God will send a Savior
HUMAN GOVERNMENT—I must value humans as God does
MORAL RESPONSIBILITY—I must choose to serve or reject God
INNOCENCE—I am a sinner; I am not innocent before God
GENERAL REVELATION—I know God is real, eternal and holy

You see, God was preparing the Jews, and the rest of the world, for a Redeemer—that was the fourth dispensation, the Promise—a personal Savior, Jesus Christ. He would be the ultimate revelation of God, an *exact representation,* according to Hebrews 1:3. By this point in history, God's chosen people, the Jews, knew a lot about their Creator, the Master of the house. And the Master was about to send down a living, breathing, *exact representation* of himself, so they could see him in person! Everything God did for us, from building this magnificent house and moving us around in it, trying to get our attention, all of it led to this great moment in history: when God's very own Son, Jesus, being one with God, would humble himself to take on a human body and live in the house with us! God carved his love motif into this house for us—it is everywhere. He has given us more and more information about himself, leading us and wooing us to him. He called out a small group of people to demonstrate a proper relationship with him, so that we might be jealous and come looking for him. And finally, he sent Jesus, who is one with God, to come into the house and live with us.

This was always part of the plan. As stated earlier, many people believe, mistakenly, that God created humans, and when humans sinned, God had to figure out what to do about it. Wrong. God's plan was proactive, not reactive. The plan of redemption was in place **before** creation. Revelation 13:8 speaks of the *Lamb that was slain from the creation of the world.* It was God's plan to send Jesus into the world, before there was a world. Jesus was always involved in the big picture—the house we've been referring to—the plan of redemption that included creation. In fact, Jesus was intimately involved in creation. John 1:3 says, *Through him (Jesus) all things were made; without him nothing was made that has been made.*

Jesus was involved in creating this great plan. He was involved in creating the heavens and the earth, all of its people, the people to whom he knew he would come live with someday. He knew he would one day humble himself, leave the glory of living above creation and enter it, take on all its weaknesses, just to show humanity what God is really, really like. John 1:1 refers to Jesus as the *Word*, an English translation of the Greek word "logos." Logos can mean "intent, reasoning, or motive." In other words, God intended to redeem us. He was motivated to save us, and Jesus embodied that intention, that motive. He embodied God's reasoning. What's more, he knew he would be rejected by most people, knew that he would be sacrificed, but he came and did it anyway. He did it to put things back as they should be, the way God intended things to be; the way things were before we humans disobeyed. Let's review what we have covered so far.

The General Revelation—all humans recognize the reality of God, that he is eternal and divine

Dispensation of Innocence—the awareness of evil, though not yet the experience of evil

Dispensation of Moral Responsibility—there is a God who is righteous and holy, and he has an enemy, Satan. I must choose one or the other

Dispensation of Human Government—God values humans and considers our lives sacred, so we are accountable to one another for how we treat each other

Dispensation of Promise—a Redeemer is coming to put everything back the way it should be

Dispensation of the Law—shows us our guilt, from God's point of view, and prepares us to accept the Redeemer

Dispensation of Grace—the Church Age...........

This isn't just where we happen to be on the tour of this great house built by our Creator. This is also where we happen to be right now in human history. There are five dispensations behind us, each one building on the other, giving us more and more information about God, more and more revelation, leading to this current church age. There is one future dispensation, but we will cover that later.

The truth about sovereignty is simple: God is sovereign. He is supreme. He is above all others in status, rank, and character. He created everything that exists. The secret to understanding the truth about God's sovereignty is in knowing **why** he is sovereign. Hopefully you now have a greater understanding of why God is sovereign, and how we are to respond to that. The other four truths depend entirely on the fact of God's sovereignty.

PART ONE REVIEW

Terms to Remember:

SOVEREIGNTY—God is in charge

GENERAL REVELATION—God has revealed himself to us through his creation

DISPENSATION—God has revealed more about himself throughout history

INNOCENCE—Adam and Eve were innocent until they chose to disobey

MORAL RESPONSIBILITY—Loss of innocence meant Cain and Abel had to choose to serve God in faith or reject what they knew about him

HUMAN GOVERNMENT—God taught us how he values human life so we could live in peace with each other

PROMISE—God let us know he would provide Someone to live up to his standards on our behalf. Jesus Christ is that Someone.

THE LAW—God showed us his standards and helped us see that we cannot live up to them. We need Someone to do that for us.

Points:
- **THERE IS ONLY ONE TRUE GOD**
- **GOD'S POWER IS ETERNAL AND HIS NATURE IS DIVINE (HOLY)**
- **GOD IS PERSONAL**
- **GOD IS A HERO**
- **SALVATION IS A GIFT**

Questions to think about:
1. WHY DO BAD THINGS HAPPEN TO GOOD PEOPLE?
2. DID THE PEOPLE WHO DIED IN THE FLOOD DESERVE PUNISHMENT?
3. IS CAPITAL PUNISHMENT FAIR?
4. WHAT PURPOSE DO THE JEWISH PEOPLE SERVE IN GOD'S PLAN OF REDEMPTION?

PART TWO

THE
TRUTH
ABOUT
SALVATION

CHAPTER THREE

WHERE SALVATION BEGINS

I gladly gave my life to Christ when I was nine years old. And while I certainly did not understand all the ramifications of being a Christian, one thing was absolutely certain in my mind: God initiated the relationship. He was calling me! Honestly, at that moment, it didn't really matter what he was calling me to, calling me for, or calling me out of. God was trying to get my attention, and I wanted to give him my attention right then. I had been in Sunday School all my life, knew the Bible stories, and knew that God loved me and sent his Son Jesus Christ to die for my sins. I knew a lot **about** God before he spoke to me, but when he spoke to me, I **knew** him. It became personal that day, sitting in the pew of my home church.

Point: God initiated our relationship when he devised his plan of redemption. He initiated by making himself known. He initiated by sending Christ. The Bible teaches that salvation belongs to God. You cannot save yourself.

Of course, I wasn't the only kid in that church. In fact, I grew up watching dozens of young people march down the aisle to "get saved." We grew up together, all of us, going to the same schools and the same church. We learned the same Bible verses, went on the same youth retreats, and participated in all the same church programs, but the results were not always the same. Seventeen years after I was saved, there was a moment of clarity for me one Sunday morning sitting in the worship service of that same church. I mentioned this back in Chapter One, talking about the fog. Moments of clarity were rare, but that day I looked around the sanctuary. It suddenly occurred to me, that of all the people I grew up with in that church, I was the only one still there. I was the only one still active in that church, and could only think of one or two who attended church anywhere. Something about that seemed terribly wrong.

No, I didn't pat myself on the back for sticking with it, or being the exception to the rule. Remember, I was trying to navigate through the fog, fully aware that we, the church, including me, were missing something, and people were wandering from their faith because of it. I was broken-hearted by what I saw around me, how the transformational gospel didn't seem to be transforming people, at least not permanently. Back then, I didn't know what we were missing. Today, I know that we were missing the **truth about Salvation**.

Term to Remember: SALVATION means we can be delivered from sin and its penalty. God provides that deliverance for us because he loves us.

You see, I grew up in a time when it was easy to "become" a Christian. Sermon after sermon from pastors and evangelists explained, often in frightening detail, how utterly awful hell is. The pain, torture, flames, and torment that lasted for all eternity. "If you don't want to go to hell, you must be saved!" was the call I heard over and over. All you had to do to avoid hell was to walk down the aisle and talk to the preacher. At least it seemed that way. Sadly, it is true what they said about hell. It is awful. It's not a place where God wants any of us to go. He didn't create hell for us. Matthew 25:41 says, *Then he will say to those on his left, "Depart from me, you who are cursed, into the eternal fire prepared for the devil and his angels."*

Remember our analogy from Part One, about the house God built? God is a Creator, but Satan is a destroyer. God demands order, but Satan introduced chaos into the house. Satan rebelled against God and successfully tempted the first humans to also rebel. God is putting things back as they should be, and will, on his time schedule, return his house to a holy, orderly place. Hell was prepared for Satan because there is simply no place in God's holy, orderly house for an unholy, disorderly rebel. When God wraps up human history, there must be someplace for Satan to go. God had no choice but to prepare some eternal place for Satan and his followers, and one day God will put them there for good. *And the devil, who deceived them, was thrown into the lake of burning sulphur, where the beast (antichrist) and the false prophet had been thrown. They will be tormented day and night forever and ever--*Revelation 20:10.

For me, the thing that makes hell so awful is the total and complete absence there of God. We know that God created the universe with his own fingerprints all over it, imbued with his character, and he said it was very good. Now imagine how God felt about preparing a place that was not good, not pleasing to him, a place devoid of his character and his love. It is a place God never wanted to create, but he had to, because he is going to put his house back in order. Now imagine how God feels about any human being, which he created and loves, going to spend their eternity in hell. God's wrath is real and justified, and many will feel it for eternity, but it is not the way God wants it.

Hell is a reality that must be taught and understood. However, as an incentive to become a Christian, I find it lacking. Hell is a place of punishment, and no one wants to be punished. Ask anyone on the street if he/she would like to spend eternity in suffering torment, and I'm sure almost everyone would answer, "No, of course not!" The desire to avoid punishment is not a spiritual desire—it is a natural, cognitive desire.

WHERE SALVATION BEGINS

Salvation begins with God. *Salvation belongs to our God, who sits on the throne, and to the Lamb--*Revelation 7:10. Salvation was God's idea, his plan. 2 Peter 3:9 teaches us that God is....*not wanting anyone to perish, but everyone to come to repentance.* Remember some important points from Chapter One: God wants your attention. He wants you to seek him out. He wants to be found. God wants a relationship with you. God loves you.

There are, however, some obstacles to overcome. First of all, just like Adam and Eve, our sin nature makes us spiritually dead. You cannot overcome that death without Christ's intervention. As I mentioned earlier, the fear of hell is not a spiritual reaction to truth, but a cognitive reaction. The spirit of the unbeliever is dead, but his body is alive. His mind is alive. He can be aware of God's existence, and choose to seek God or turn away. If the fear of hell prompts humanity to seek God's help, then I say, "Hallelujah!" But we must be careful not to stop there. We must move beyond the cognitive and into the spiritual. Therein lies the second obstacle. Satan works hard to keep people from getting to this point, the point of true salvation. 2 Corinthians 4:3-4 find Paul teaching this truth, *And even if our gospel is veiled, it is veiled to those who are perishing. The god of this age (Satan) has blinded the minds of unbelievers, so that they cannot see the light of the gospel of the glory of Christ, who is the image of God.*

God has revealed himself to man through creation (Romans 1:19-20) so that all men know (cognitively) that God exists, is righteous, and is eternal. It is his desire that man will (cognitively) reach out for him (Acts 17:27). This is man's movement toward God, but it is not spiritual yet. Remember, God initiated the whole plan of redemption by revealing himself to man. God beckons us through what we see and know about him. When man seeks God and reaches out for him, God's Spirit can then initiate the spiritual aspect of the meeting, removing Satan's blinders and opening the spiritual eyes of the man. If he accepts the offer initiated by the Holy Spirit, he is saved. Though he was spiritually dead, he is spiritually resurrected through Christ.

Let me be clear on one point. When I say this is man's initiation, remember that Acts 17 is explaining how God has worked in human history to lead us towards him. God initiated the plan of salvation. Humans did not. While we were spiritually dead, God was very much alive and working to overcome that obstacle for us. However, God does not force his will upon us. He leads us, so that we will *perhaps reach out for him.* I quoted 2 Corinthians 4:3-4 two paragraphs back. Now consider verse 6 of that same chapter, *For God, who said, "Let light shine out of darkness," made his light shine in our hearts to give us the light of the knowledge of the glory of God in the face of Christ.* God wants your attention. He wants you to seek him out. He wants to be found. God wants a relationship with you. God loves you.

The truth about salvation is that even if you are looking for God, you cannot come to him on your terms or your schedule. Only God's Spirit can initiate your salvation. I am convinced that one big problem in the church I grew up in and the church of today is that far too many people have walked down the aisle and made a **cognitive** choice to follow Jesus, but not a spiritual choice. Many have made a rational, natural decision to become a Christian, without realizing that the Holy Spirit had not yet opened the spiritual door.

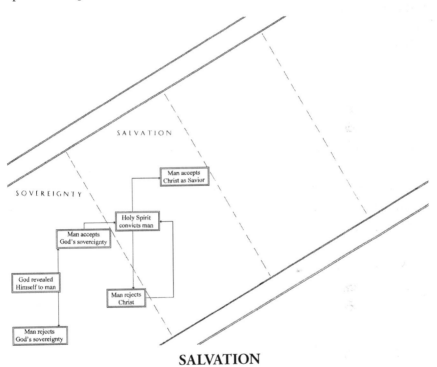

SALVATION

I once invited a coworker to a revival service at the church I was involved in. He professed Christianity, but not very convincingly. During the invitation, it was obvious that he was struggling, and I felt he was under very heavy conviction. I asked if he wanted me to pray with him. He was crying quietly, holding on to the back of the pew with his head down, his entire body under stress. But he politely said no. The next day at work, he stopped me and asked me this question. "If I got saved years ago just to get my fire insurance, am I really saved, or am I going to hell?" I answered, "If you walked the aisle and went through the motions just because you thought it would get you into heaven, then no, it probably wasn't genuine." He just looked at me and said, "That's what I thought."

The look on his face told me everything that was going on inside of him. He knew, deep down, that he had not been transformed by the gospel. He knew that becoming a Christian should be more profound than just a cognitive choice—"Heaven or hell? I'll take heaven!" And yet, many people never move beyond the cognitive curiosity about God into the life-altering pursuit of him. I am convinced it's because no one leads them there.

Jesus had something to say about it, and it's recorded in Matthew 7:13-14, *Enter through the narrow gate. For wide is the gate and broad is the road that leads to destruction, and many enter through it. But small is the gate and narrow the road that leads to life, and only a few find it.* Many readers like to interpret the broad road as simply the road of life itself, a road that every single human travels. The narrow road, of course, would be the road to salvation. I don't think this was at all what Jesus was teaching. I think Jesus was teaching that the broad road is what people **think** is the road to salvation. They think they're on the right road. They think they are saved. These aren't people just traveling through life—on the contrary, these are people who think they have found the road to eternal life in heaven, be it through good works, being a good person, attending church, or getting their "fire insurance." They want to be saved, but they are on the wrong road, the wide road, and don't even realize it. Jesus was telling us the horrible truth that most people who think they are saved are really not. Only a few people will actually find the truth about salvation, a salvation that transforms you. Let Jesus' words sink in for a moment: *Only a few find it.*

Here's a point that makes this teaching even sadder: my coworker apparently realized he was on the wrong road, the broad one, but refused to change course. I believe the Holy Spirit was convicting him about true salvation, but he resisted, maybe because he was starting to understand that God expected more from him than just lip service. God was asking for a serious relationship, and my coworker did not want to make that kind of commitment. When you realize that God is sovereign, you also realize that you are not. Salvation takes on a wholly new meaning. It becomes much more than just a get-out-of-hell-free card. It becomes a yielding of your will to God's will. That's the problem with seeing salvation as fire insurance. It is a selfish pursuit of redemption, one that would protect the "insured" from punishment, but still allow him to continue living recklessly.

Point: Remember Cain? God did not accept his offerings—his worship—because God knew his heart wasn't in it. Cain was trying to appease God to avoid punishment. It was a natural act of worship, not a spiritual act of worship.

In the real world, insurance companies expect their customers to maintain certain standards of behavior. If you own a car, and you drive it, you must have it insured. Suppose you called your insurance agent and asked this question, "If I wreck my car while driving 120 mph down a country road while reading a magazine behind the wheel, will you cover the damages?" I think you would be looking for another insurance agent. If you insist on behaving in a way that is contradictory to their standards, contradictory to the law and common sense, why should they cover you? No rational person would expect them to take that risk. So why would you ask God to make sure you get into heaven when you die, but allow you to live a life that is contradictory to his standards, his law, and common sense? The "salvation as insurance plan" just doesn't work. If I choose Christ only for the benefits to me, then I am only glorifying myself—Jesus is not glorified.

CHAPTER FOUR

SOVEREIGNTY AND SALVATION MERGE

Years ago, I was confronted by some teaching on the doctrine of election that was pretty extreme. This is the place where the truth about God's sovereignty and the truth about God's salvation merge, or collide, depending on your viewpoint. Let me explain before we go any farther on our study of salvation.

The doctrine of election, sometimes called predestination, is currently a hotly debated topic in evangelical churches. Romans 8:29 says, *For those God foreknew he also predestined to be conformed to the likeness of his son, that he might be the firstborn among many brothers.* Those who take this predestination point to the extreme usually cite the sovereignty of God as the foundation for their beliefs. If you read Part One of this book, then you know I feel very strongly about God being absolutely sovereign. The merger, or collision, occurs in determining whether or not God's sovereignty allows man to choose salvation, or if it is chosen for him.

Term to remember: PREDESTINATION means that God decided certain things in advance. For example, God decided to redeem mankind before he actually created us. What else God decided in advance is subject to debate.

Some of my friends claim that before God created man he chose certain among us to be saved, thus he foreknew **those and those only** and predestined them for salvation. Of course, this interpretation would necessarily mean that God did **not** choose everyone else, and therefore everyone else was **chosen**, by default, for hell. I know, some of you are grimacing at the thought, but I have heard Christians say that God made some people for damnation so the rest of us would appreciate salvation. That is, admittedly, the most extreme version of the doctrine of election I have ever been exposed to, and I reject it flatly. We already covered in Part One the fact that hell was prepared *for the devil and his angels*, not for humans.

In 2 Thessalonians, the apostle Paul is teaching about the end-times, things yet to happen, and he refers to the lost as *those who are perishing.* Chapter 2:10. He goes on to say this: *They perish because they refused to love the truth and so be saved.* It does not say they perish because they weren't chosen. I have found no teaching in the scripture that some people are predestined to hell. Paul says emphatically that they perish because they reject the truth. We learned in Part One that there are certain truths about God which he has made plain to everyone.

When I recall Acts 17, which tells us God has intervened in human history in order that we might seek him and reach out for him, I must reject the notion that God only chose a few for salvation. Verses 26-28 of that chapter states *from one man he made every nation of men, that they should inhabit the whole earth; and he determined the times set for them and the exact places where they should live. God did this so that men would seek him and perhaps reach out for him, though he is not far from each one of us. For in him we live and move and have our being.* If we take this passage literally, then God has intervened on behalf of all humanity.

My friends have said to me, "Dead men can't look for God!" They are, of course, assuming that salvation begins in the spiritual, and they are ignoring the cognitive. While the lost human is spiritually dead, he still has a pulse and brain activity. He is physically alive and the general revelation is designed to appeal to his physical senses. It is only **after** salvation, according to 2 Corinthians 5:7, that *we live by faith and not by sight.* Faith is not mystical or magical. Faith is simply accepting spiritual truths in spite of our cognitive limitations. Remember what Jesus said in Matthew 7 about the narrow path and the small gate, that only a few would find it? Why would Jesus lament the fact that so few would find salvation if only a few were chosen to be saved in the first place? And why would God only choose a few? These two passages from 2 Corinthians and Matthew present a major hurdle for those who take an extreme view of predestination.

There is another passage often used to support an extreme view. Ephesians 1:4-6 says, *For he chose us in him before the creation of the world to be holy and blameless in his sight. In love he predestined us to be adopted as his sons through Jesus Christ, in accordance with his pleasure and will—to the praise of his glorious grace, which he has freely given us in the One he loves.* How you deal with this merging of sovereignty and salvation depends on how you interpret verse 4. Does the "us" refer only to Christians, or to all of humanity?

If you say it refers only to the chosen few, then you can't interpret Acts 17 or Matthew 7 literally. You have to find some other explanation for those. If the Acts passage really means that God intervened in human history on behalf of the chosen few and not all of humanity, then that interpretation creates another contradiction for the extreme view: it would still mean that the chosen are expected to *seek him and perhaps reach out for him.* If you say the "us" in Ephesians 1:4 refers to all of humanity, then you don't have to reinterpret other scriptures to fit. God chose all of humanity for the same purpose—to be holy and blameless. Go back to Genesis 1:26, Then God said, *"Let us make man in our image, in our likeness, and let them rule over the fish of the sea and the birds of the air, over the livestock, over all the earth, and over all the creatures that move along the ground."* Notice God did not say "let us make man in our image and choose **some from among him** to rule...."

We are the only creatures God made who carry his image—we are his image bearers in this universe. He made us in his likeness and gave us dominion over all the rest of creation. Stop and think about that for a moment. God does not distinguish here two types of humans, noble or ignoble, elect or damned, chosen or not chosen. If God made some, or I should say most, humans for damnation, then why would he make them to bear his image and his likeness and give them authority over his created world? Is it God's will for his image to be represented in hell? How does

God receive glory by giving such honor to humans who were created for dishonor? Frankly, it makes no sense to me, and only creates fog where the scripture is actually quite straightforward.

Consider the words of Peter, addressing the concerns of some first-century Christians that Christ was slow in returning. He said, *The Lord is not slow in keeping his promise, as some understand slowness. He is patient with you, not wanting anyone to perish, but everyone to come to repentance.* 2 Peter 3:9. If you believe the Ephesians passage (*For he chose us in him…*) only refers to the chosen few, then you must assume the same of the 2 Peter passage, that Peter means God is waiting for all the chosen ones to be saved. In other words, if he comes too soon, some of the elect will be lost and won't come to repentance. But if God forces his will on the elect, and for them grace is irresistible, as some teach, then why the need for patience? The extreme view assumes that Peter is talking about the chosen ones who have not yet heard the gospel, but his letter clearly addresses the church, those who are presumed saved already. It seems logical that Peter is talking to Christians who are not very patient. Many Christians today are not patient.

Peter is encouraging impatient Christians to have patience, because although they are anxious to be united with their Savior, God is reluctant to close the age of grace, the church age, because **it is not His will for humans to perish.** God does not find pleasure in you, or anyone else being unholy or full of blame. His pleasure and will is for humans to be holy and blameless, and he sent Christ to make us holy and blameless. The sad fact is, however, that most will choose the wrong path, just as Jesus said they would.

A point must be made concerning the *praise of his glorious grace,* from the Ephesians passage, Chapter 1, verse 6. A grace that is flatly denied to most of humanity does not seem glorious. If you consider yourself to be among the chosen few, then I suppose it might seem glorious to you, but how would the rest of God's creation view it? Let me make this more personal. When I was first confronted by the extreme view of the doctrine of election, I must confess that it rattled me. I was young, and had not been well-taught, and this new teaching was coming from friends whom I otherwise trusted. The idea that I was chosen did not make me feel special—on the contrary, it made me feel very uncomfortable.

So I did what I always do when I need an answer—I got on my face in the floor and asked God about it. I remember clearly asking him to show me if indeed only a few were even offered the opportunity to be called his children. God spoke to me, not in an audible voice, but through his Spirit. He simply asked me this: "John, what have I always been to you?" I answered him out loud, "You have proven yourself to be a loving Father, just like you claim in your bible." He replied, "Then why would I be different to anyone else?" It is anecdotal evidence for sure, and I cannot prove that God spoke to me, but his answer was logical. God refers to himself in scripture as a loving Father, because no matter what kind of household you were raised in, we all know what a loving Father **should** be. We know instinctively that fathers who love us also protect us, nurture us, and discipline us. We know that any man who fathers several children and chooses to show his love and grace to only some of them is not what we consider a loving father. If God created most humans for hell, then those rejected humans would have legitimate reason to argue his claims to be a loving Father.

There is one more passage of scripture that must be addressed. Those who hold an extreme view of election often refer to Romans 9. Verses 16-18 say, *It does not, therefore, depend on man's desire or effort, but on God's mercy. For the scripture says to Pharaoh: "I raised you up for this very purpose, that I might display my power in you and that my name might be proclaimed in all the earth." Therefore God has mercy on whom he wants to have mercy, and he hardens whom he wants to harden.* First of all, you must read all of Romans and understand the context. Much of what Paul writes here addresses the concerns of Jewish Christians who are jealous that Gentiles are being offered and are receiving the gospel of Jesus Christ. Most Jews rejected Christ, even though they were God's chosen people, and many Gentiles accepted Christ, even though they were not God's chosen. Also, consider the word "raised" in verse 17. The original Greek means "to rouse fully." Since that verse is quoted from Exodus 9:16, you can also look at the Hebrew word that is rendered "raised," and it means "to stand" or "appoint." It has a similar connotation to the word God used in Genesis 17:5, when he said of Abraham, *I have made you a father or many nations.*

Point: God did not *create* Abraham as a father, but *appointed* him to become one. God raised him up to be a father. Abraham, having the freedom to choose, made the choice to obey God's calling on his life. Thus he became a father, even in his old age.

In other words, it does not appear likely that God **created** Pharaoh for damnation or destruction or even for disobedience. This was Pharaoh's choice all along, but by appointing Pharaoh to a certain task, God proved that he can use even those who hate him to complete his plan of redemption. Did God really harden Pharaoh's heart? Certainly. God did not put in his heart the desire to go against God and his plan. Pharaoh had already made that choice. God simply gave him a stronger dose of the medicine he already desired, and in so doing, proved to his people, the Jews, that he could and would do exactly what he promised.

Point: God can and will use you to accomplish his purpose. It is your choice to be used in obedience or in disobedience, but God is sovereign. Even when you make the wrong choice and think you are acting independently, you are still operating within the limits of God's sovereign will.

It also got the attention of the Egyptians. It is always God's intention that humans recognize his existence (General Revelation), recognize their lack of innocence (1st Dispensation), and their moral responsibility to choose him or his enemy (2nd Dispensation). Remember that even the Egyptians were descended from Adam, and they would have had this basic knowledge of God. However, as Romans 1:21 points out, the Egyptians, and most of the world, were guilty, *for although they knew God, they neither glorified him as God nor gave thanks to him, but their thinking became futile and their foolish hearts were darkened.* That obviously included Pharaoh. But consider the next two verses in Romans 1: *Although they claimed to be wise, they became fools and exchanged the glory of the immortal God for images made to look like mortal man and birds and animals and reptiles.* If you have any knowledge of ancient Egypt and their religious beliefs, you know how they replaced the worship of the Creator with the worship of creatures.

CHAPTER FIVE

WHERE SALVATION LEADS

True salvation is a covenant relationship. Remember Abraham, from Chapter Two? We talked in that chapter about the fourth dispensation, the Promise, and how God called Abraham to be the father of many descendants. These descendants, according to God, would become a great nation and a blessing to the whole world. That promise was a covenant between God and Abraham, initiated by God. God told him, according to Genesis 17:4-5, *as for me, this is my covenant with you: you will be called the father of many nations. No longer will you be called Abram; your name will be Abraham, for I have made you a father of many nations.*

Term to Remember: A COVENANT is a binding agreement between two parties. When God makes a covenant he is promising to do something.

God spoke to Abraham. God initiated the covenant. God called him to be part of his plan of redemption. Abraham accepted the terms of the covenant—an act of obedience—circumcision for him and his descendants. Now, I have to say here, many people find this an odd thing for God to tell someone to do. You must understand, the covenant, God's promise to Abraham, was that he and his wife, in their old age and with no children, would be the start of a large people group, the Jews. God promised to give this barren couple many children, grandchildren, and so on. But more importantly, God was going to bring the promised Redeemer into the world through this same group of people. Jesus, Son of God, would take on human flesh as a Jew, a direct descendant of this seemingly now-barren couple.

Circumcision was an act of obedience to the covenant, but also a sign of the covenant. It was a sign of a physical change, something tangible, and yet it was private, between the Jew and God. It was not readily apparent to the public. Circumcision did not serve as a public witness that the circumcised man was in a covenant relationship with God. His obedience to God's law was his public witness. God distinguished this fact during a time of Israel's disobedience. He said, through his prophet Jeremiah, that *even the whole house of Israel is uncircumcised in heart.* Jeremiah 9:26

Romans 2:25 addresses this issue. *Circumcision has value if you observe the law, but if you break the law, you have become as though you had not been circumcised.* Circumcision was the Old Testament equivalent of a cognitive choice, but honoring God's laws in your daily life was deeper, more profound. It was a spiritual act of worship, not physical. It was a surrendering of one's lifestyle. It proved to others that the Jew was serious about being one of God's chosen evangelists, part of his plan of redemption. The Jewish people, who became the nation of Israel, were called by God to show the rest of the world what a true and meaningful relationship with God looked like. Their obedience to God was essential, not just so they could receive God's blessings, but so the rest of the world could be blessed through them so that men would *hear of your great name and your mighty hand and your outstretched arm.* Outstretched arm! Being obedient to God, being holy people, being transformed and different from the rest of the world, would show others that God wanted a relationship with them. It would show them that his arm is outstretched, waiting for them to come looking. Obedience to God was the first step in being an evangelist. That's why salvation can never be just about you getting your fire insurance. It can never be just about you escaping hell and punishment. God is calling humans to salvation **and** holiness. Salvation should lead us to holiness. It should transform us and change us. When it doesn't, it means one of two things. Either the new Christian is not being taught and discipled, or his salvation experience was purely cognitive and not spiritual. In other words, a Christian who is not transformed by the power of Christ's gospel is either an immature Christian or not one at all. Salvation should lead to transformation.

TRANSFORMATION

Therefore, I urge you, brothers, in view of God's mercy, to offer your bodies as living sacrifices, holy and pleasing to God—this is your spiritual act of worship. Do not conform any longer to the pattern of this world, but be transformed by the renewing of your mind. Then you will be able to test and approve what God's will is—his good, pleasing and perfect will. Romans 12: 1-2. When I was trying to navigate my way out of the fog, this scripture nagged me. I knew my mind had not been transformed. I wanted to offer my physical self as a living sacrifice, but failed more often than not. Spiritual maturity like that seemed difficult, maybe even impossible. It seemed that God was calling me to something unachievable, an unattainable goal.

I had never been taught that there were steps to take in my walk with Jesus. The way it was explained to me made spiritual maturity seem like something that would just happen without much effort, as if each new Christian went on auto-pilot. The problem was, it just wasn't happening much, not to me or most people I knew. Again, our Christian community just seemed to be living in a fog.

It was sad to watch people, including myself, struggling with the same sins over and over again, never achieving much victory over them. Eventually many quit trying, because it seemed futile. Auto-pilot was failing us—we were going down in flames at an alarming rate.

God did break through my foggy ignorance with one important clue from this passage of scripture. It said, *be transformed*. It did not say "you will be transformed," as if, "oh yeah; after you are saved you will automatically become mature." It said *be transformed*, as if to imply, "you must make sure this happens!" That was another great moment of clarity for me: I was responsible for growing up!

God had made a covenant with Abraham and the Jewish people, to be his representatives in the world. Circumcision was a physical act of obedience to the covenant, but obedience to God's laws was, for them, a spiritual act of obedience, a spiritual act of worship. It meant sacrificing your own agenda for God's. But God promised them a new, better covenant. Christ would usher in this new covenant, when God said *I will put my law in their minds and write it on their hearts.* Jeremiah 31:33. This is why Romans 12:1-2 tells us that offering our bodies as living sacrifices is a spiritual act of worship. By offering your body to God, you are asking him to put his law in your mind and write it on your heart. You are sacrificing your own agenda and surrendering your body to God's laws! You are giving him permission to reprogram your mind and heart, to think godly and not ungodly.

Christ died for your sins and mine, but he did so much more than that. He made it possible for the law to be internalized. The old covenant was centered on the conduct of the Jew, but the new covenant would center on the character of the Christian.

If you study the Old Testament, you will see that the Jewish people had a long history of disobedience. Let's face it, obedience is hard. That is why God promised reward (blessing) for obedience and punishment (suffering) for disobedience. Obedience was often motivated by fear, and still it was hard to obey consistently. Children are often obedient because they are afraid of being punished, but hopefully they grow up and develop the kind of inner character that makes them want to do the right thing. Character is a better motivator than fear. The difference between the old and new covenants would be that character construction would be easier. This is why Israel longed so desperately for the Promise, the Redeemer, to come. Again, consider Jeremiah 31, verse 33, where God said, *I will put my law in their minds and write it on their hearts.* Another promise from God in verse 34: *For I will forgive their wickedness and will remember their sins no more.*

So this promised Redeemer, Jesus, was going to bring a new covenant, where God would internalize his law, making obedience easier, and deal with the sin problem once and for all. Hallelujah! Jesus proclaimed the new covenant to his disciples at the Lord's Supper. Luke 22:20 says, *In the same way, after the supper he took the cup, saying, "This cup is the new covenant in my blood, which is poured out for you."*

Jesus' death and resurrection, his sacrifice, ushered in a new dispensation, the **Church Age**, or age of grace, and an entirely new way of relating to God.

How did God internalize the law? That is the work of the Holy Spirit. Jesus explained it, and it is recorded in John 16:7, *But I tell you the truth: it is for your good that I am going away. Unless I go away, the Counselor will not come to you; but if I go, I will send him to you.*

When you are saved and begin to follow Jesus, something truly spectacular happens. The Spirit of God takes up residence in your soul. To really understand this, we need to take another look at the old covenant. As mentioned before, the Jewish people were called to be obedient to God, a holy nation, so that they could show the world what a relationship with the One True God looked like. But there was another reason why God demanded holiness of his people. He wanted to dwell with them. Remember from Part One, Solomon's prayer from 1 Kings 8, at the dedication of the temple in Jerusalem, where he asked God to respond to the prayers of foreigners? That great temple had a predecessor, called the tabernacle. The tabernacle was built by the Jewish people while Moses was leading them through the wilderness, before they became a sovereign nation. They built the tabernacle according to God's instructions, and Exodus 40:34-35 tell us, *Then the cloud covered the Tent of Meeting, and the glory of the Lord filled the tabernacle. Moses could not enter the Tent of Meeting because the cloud had settled upon it, and the glory of the Lord filled the tabernacle.*

Ever since the first humans sinned against God, he has been implementing his prearranged plan of redemption, slowly but surely bringing us closer and closer to the fellowship that Adam and Eve enjoyed in the garden. God is a holy God, and he demanded holiness from his chosen people group, the Israelites, so that he could descend and dwell with them. Even when they were living in tents, God had Moses build him a tent to dwell in!

The tabernacle was made up of three parts. The outer part, or court, was the place for sacrifices to be made. (The temple built by Solomon added a fourth part, the court of the Gentiles. That's what Solomon referred to in his dedication prayer, where he asked God to answer the prayers of foreigners who came there seeking God. Non-Jews were not allowed past that point.) The inner part was divided in two: the Holy Place, where only the priests could go in, and Most Holy Place, where only the high priest could enter, once a year, to make atonement for the people's sins. It was in this inner, Most Holy Place, sometimes called the Holy of Holies, that the glory of the Lord settled. God came and dwelt in a tent, just to be close to his people.

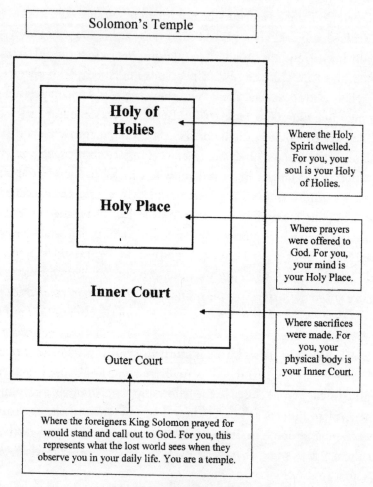

Solomon's Temple

Holy of Holies

Where the Holy Spirit dwelled. For you, your soul is your Holy of Holies.

Holy Place

Where prayers were offered to God. For you, your mind is your Holy Place.

Inner Court

Where sacrifices were made. For you, your physical body is your Inner Court.

Outer Court

Where the foreigners King Solomon prayed for would stand and call out to God. For you, this represents what the lost world sees when they observe you in your daily life. You are a temple.

TEMPLE

So back to the question, how did God internalize the law? Your body is like that outer part. That's why God tells you to give your body as a living sacrifice. Just as the Jewish worshiper went into the outer court to make sacrifices to God, your body becomes a living sacrifice to him, surrendered to him. This is your spiritual act of worship. Your mind, which contains your will, is like the inner part, the Holy Place. That is why God tells you to renew your mind. This is where Jesus does his character building in you. This is where God puts his law in your mind and writes it on your heart. Your soul is like that second inner part, the Most Holy Place. When you ask Jesus to save you, the Holy Spirit of God comes and settles in your soul, in your Holy of Holies.

Under the old covenant, God demanded holy living in order for him to come and dwell. God does not make that demand in the new covenant, at least in the sense that he demands you clean up your life before he will save you. No, he takes you as-is. However, the scripture clearly teaches that God does demand holy living once he takes up residence in your Holy of Holies. Jesus called him the Counselor because he convicts you, guides you, counsels you in holy living. The Bible is still critical to your walk with Christ. You must read it and study it faithfully, but as a Christian, when you read and study God's Word, the Spirit aids your understanding. The Spirit living in you confirms and affirms that which is outside of you. The Spirit intercedes for you. Consider Romans 8:26, *In the same way, the Spirit helps us in our weakness. We do not know what we ought to pray for, but the Spirit himself intercedes for us with groans that words cannot express.*

This is a huge benefit that old covenant saints did not have. Once Jesus was sacrificed on the cross, our sins were atoned for, but the Spirit of God was free to come and inhabit the Christian. The law was no longer just something to hold in your hands—it was internalized. The soul of man, once dead, is now resurrected and becomes a holy place. Your body, once a mausoleum for your dead soul, is gloriously transformed into a throne room of God Almighty! 1 Corinthians 6:19-20 says, *Do you not know that your body is a temple of the Holy Spirit, who is in you, whom you have received from God? You are not your own; you were bought at a price. Therefore honor God with your body.*

This is why no one should want or expect "fire insurance" Christianity. It is not real. It does not transform. True salvation not only alters your future status, assuring you a place in heaven, but it alters your current status. You are permanently changed by the presence of the Holy Spirit in your soul. This is the truth about salvation

PART TWO REVIEW

Terms to Remember:
SALVATION—God saving us from sin and its penalty
PREDESTINATION—the things God determined to happen in advance
COVENANT—a binding agreement

Points:
- **GOD INITIATES SALVATION**
- **CAIN WAS SEEKING "FIRE INSURANCE"**
- **ABRAHAM CHOSE TO OBEY GOD'S CALLING**
- **YOUR CHOICE TO OBEY OR DISOBEY GOD DOES NOT MEAN THAT YOU OVERRIDE THE SOVEREIGNTY OF GOD**

PART THREE

THE
TRUTH
ABOUT
SANCTITY

CHAPTER SIX

CONFESSION AND REPENTANCE

God didn't call me to the ministry until I was thirty years old. I spent the first twelve years of my adult life confused, as far as knowing what I was supposed to be doing with my life. Since my father was a builder, I naturally inherited an interest in building things, especially if I had the chance to design them. There is something fascinating, to me anyway, about drawing a house on paper and then seeing it rise up from the ground. So I studied drafting and went into the business, though it never seemed to click for me. I survived, but never thrived. I had big dreams and visions, but they never worked out the way I imagined.

When I recognized that God was calling me to the ministry, it was a little scary, but deep inside I was relieved to know my life, finally, had a purpose. I began to pray for God to lead me, and for the first year as a "minister," absolutely nothing happened! At least, nothing that showed to the casual observer. Some people in the ministry urged me to return to the classroom, even offering to help launch my ministry career if I did so, but when I prayed about it, God said, "no." I knew God was calling me into music ministry. Music has always been meaningful to me. I had musical training, and had played the organ in my home church from the time I was sixteen until I was twenty-seven. Singing was also something I loved, and I had even led a worship service here and there. In fact, I was once asked to consider taking a position at a local church in my early twenties, but I felt no calling to the ministry then, and didn't seriously consider it.

Now, at thirty, I had the calling from God, but nobody else was calling! Nothing seemed to be happening, but God was working.

God kept telling me, in my prayer time, that it wasn't about the music—it was about connecting people with him. He assured me that he would equip me and give me whatever skills I needed, but that what I needed most was holiness. In fact, I knew God was calling me to live a level of holiness that was beyond what I had ever lived. He was calling me to a level of holiness that I thought was impossible. Remember, I had not been taught very well, and so I just assumed holy living, sanctity, was something that just magically happened if you were really a Christian. And up to this point, I thought I was doing pretty well, at least better than most other people I knew. That was one of my biggest mistakes—comparing my holiness to others' and not to God's. I did not understand the value of confession and repentance. I knew nothing about transformation and renewal. God was telling me that, more than anything else, I needed to understand **the truth about sanctity**.

Term to Remember: SANCTITY simply means "holiness." Sanctification is a word used in church a lot and it describes the process of becoming more and more like Christ. 1 Peter 1:15-16 teaches sanctity: *But just as he who called you is holy, so be holy in all you do; for it is written: "Be holy, because I am holy."*

John 13 records a beautiful moment of Jesus' ministry to his disciples. Verses 5-10 especially give us some great insight into how we should live our lives as Christians. *After that, he poured water into a basin and began to wash his disciples' feet, drying them with the towel that was wrapped around him. He came to Simon Peter, who said to him, "Lord, are you going to wash my feet?" Jesus replied, "You do not realize now what I am doing, but later you will understand." "No," said Peter, "you shall never wash my feet." Jesus answered, "Unless I wash you, you have no part with me." "Then, Lord," Simon Peter replied, "not just my feet but my hands and my head as well!" Jesus answered, "A person who has had a bath needs only to wash his feet; his whole body is clean. And you are clean, though not every one of you."*

You already understand that taking a bath two thousand years ago was not as simple as it is today. Getting a bath and getting your body clean was a big deal. Of course, if you walk around in mostly unpaved streets with open shoes or none at all, of course your feet get dirty. That's why foot-washing was customary in the ancient world. After all, who wants to relax for dinner with dirty feet? But in this case, Jesus wasn't just being gracious and humble. He was teaching his disciples a very vital lesson about how to live their lives.

When Jesus said, *you are clean,* he was telling Peter, "You are saved." He was explaining that Peter's faith in Christ had already washed him of sin. Jesus was in the process of defeating sin and death once and for all. However, Peter needed to understand that even after he bathed and put on clean clothing, as soon as he walked outside his feet were likely to get dirty, and would soon need washing. That is true in the life of every Christian. The blood of Jesus saves you—washes you clean, and it is a bath that does not need repeating. But in the process of living life and going about your daily routine you will encounter temptation and yes, you will sin. Jesus knows that you will not be perfect this side of heaven, and he was explaining to Peter the simple lesson of confession and repentance.

As a believer and follower of Christ, you were washed, so to speak, in his sacrificial blood. *....but you were washed, you were sanctified, you were justified in the name of the Lord Jesus Christ and by the Spirit of our God* –1 Corinthians 6:11. As a Christian, you are clean, but you will not live a perfect sinless life. Jesus knows that, and that's why he offers to wash our dirty feet for us, every single day. You cannot lose your salvation. You will never need another bath from Christ. *A person who has had a bath needs only to wash his feet.* But you will need to show him your dirty feet and let him wash them for you. In other words, you must confess your sins to God on a daily basis.

Term to Remember: CONFESSION is admitting our sins to God.

This sounds so simple, yet it is probably one of the most under-taught and least understood doctrines of Christianity. Consequently, it is probably why so many Christians live such defeated lives. They have been taught that confession is a one-time event that happens when you accept Christ as Savior—that you confess you are a sinner, and then you're done confessing! Unfortunately, many Christians are walking around with feet that are filthy and disgusting, often unwilling to expose their feet to God for washing. Jesus Christ, our Sacrifice, is waiting with basin and towel; waiting for you to simply show him your feet; waiting for confession. Why does it matter so much? Because of what Jesus said to Peter: *unless I wash you, you have no part with me.* Jesus was teaching his disciples the truth about sanctity.

Sin in the life of a Christian does not cause you to lose salvation. If it did, then Jesus would have taught Peter that he would need to be bathed over and over again. Instead, he taught Peter that only his feet would need washing, but unless he allowed Jesus to do this, his fellowship with Jesus would be broken. Sin will never take away your salvation—it is secured—but sin will interrupt your fellowship with God. In Part Two, I shared my belief that many people come to Christ as a cognitive choice only, without the initiation of the Holy Spirit, and it is my belief that they are not truly saved at all if they are only seeking "fire insurance." Unfortunately, many do come to Christ as the Spirit calls and beckons, but they never learn the truth about sanctity, and they never grow in Christ the way God intends. The truth about sanctity is that God expects holiness from you, and holiness requires confession and repentance.

Term to Remember: REPENTANCE is the act of spiritually changing direction. When you recognize that you are moving away from God, repentance is the act of turning and moving towards him again.

GOD IS NOT HUMAN

Think about how you relate to others. Many times, someone will hurt or insult you, or in some other way offend you. You may confront them directly, though most people never do. Instead, it is more likely that you will simply avoid them. After all, how can you have fellowship with someone who has offended you? They may come to you and offer a sincere apology, though most people never do that either. It is more likely that they will simply avoid you. Both of you will live this way until enough time passes for you to "get over it," or for the offender to believe it no longer matters. One of you will slowly start thawing towards the other, until eventually you both ignore the offense and act as if it never even happened. No apologies will be made, and if the riff is even acknowledged, there will simply be the mutual agreement to "let bygones be bygones."

Term to Remember: RECONCILIATION means to bring things back into harmony.

That is not true reconciliation, and it doesn't erase the offense or the feelings of being offended. That's why so many relationships are so fragile, because we never truly deal with our offenses towards each other. We just act as if they never happened. We just "get over it." Unfortunately, we carry resentment and bitterness that threaten to come back up at a moment's notice. It's like being forced to swallow something that's rancid and trying to hold it down. It will upset your stomach, because your body wants to reject the rotten food. Likewise, you cannot digest bitterness and resentment. Sooner or later you will vomit it back up, and it's never pretty when that happens.

Point: We don't like to admit when we're wrong—when we're guilty. That comes from pride, and it interferes with our relationships, especially our relationship with God. If you are willing to confess and repent to God, you will find it easier to be honest with other people as well.

So what does that have to do with confession and repentance? Because we often treat God like he's human. We sin every day. We offend him, but we don't go to him and offer a sincere apology. We don't confess our offense and ask for forgiveness. If the sin is really shameful to us, we may even avoid talking to God for a while, until we think enough time has passed for him to "get over it." Then we begin to warm up to God again, and when no great punishment comes on us, we assume that the offense is forgotten and simply doesn't matter anymore. Then, of course, we can go back to business as usual, asking God to bless us and answer our prayers, and make our lives wonderful, etc.

God is holy. He is not human, and he resents being treated the way we treat other humans. Consider Psalm 50, where God is speaking to some wicked people about their sin. He says, in verse 21, *These things you have done and I kept silent; you thought I was altogether like you. But I will rebuke you and accuse you to your face.* They seemed to think that they had gotten away with their sin, that God had gotten over it, or that it just wasn't a big deal. God reminded them, and us, that he is not human, that he will not just pretend our sin never happened. In fact, he will confront our sin.

God is holy, and he doesn't just get over your sin. He hates sin, because it comes between you and him. We should never expect God to digest our rancid sin. If God could, or would, just "get over it" there would have been no need for Christ to die for our sin. God would have just forgotten about sin. And yes, while it is true that the washing Jesus gives us when we become Christians is sufficient for salvation, our daily dirtiness still needs to be dealt with in order to maintain the fellowship Christ died to provide. Our relationship with a holy God should matter enough that we seek to be clean. After all, he says, *be holy, because I am holy*—Leviticus 11:44.

Consider Jeroboam. When King Solomon died, the nation of Israel was divided. God did this because his chosen people were not being faithful to him. God promised to keep Solomon's descendants on the throne, and so he allowed Rehoboam, Solomon's son, to reign over the southern kingdom, called Judah. However, God placed Jeroboam, one of Solomon's subordinates, to reign over the northern kingdom, which kept the name Israel. A problem arose, however, because Jeroboam was afraid that the people he was governing might feel loyal to Rehoboam, because he was a descendant of Solomon and David. Plus, the temple was in the southern kingdom, and the temple represented God's presence with the Jewish people. Solomon had built the temple, and it was in Jerusalem, which David had established as the nation's capital. His concerns were understandable, except for the fact that God had already addressed the matter with him. God told Jeroboam, through the prophet Ahijah, that he was going to keep one tribe, the tribe of Judah, for David's descendants, starting with Rehoboam, to rule over in the southern kingdom. God said, however, that he would give to Jeroboam ten tribes to rule over in the northern kingdom, and told him, *If you do whatever I command you and walk in my ways and do what is right in my eyes by keeping my statutes and commands, I will be with you. I will build you a dynasty as enduring as the one I built for David and will give Israel to you. I will humble David's descendants because of this, but not forever,* 1 Kings 11:38-39.

According to God, Jeroboam and Rehoboam would rule over the two kingdoms, and God promised His blessings over Jeroboam if he would simply be obedient. In fact, God wanted to use him as a godly example for Rehoboam. God was calling Jeroboam, and the ten tribes of Jews following him, back to their role as evangelists! However, Jeroboam did not believe God. 1 Kings 12:26-27 record his concerns. Jeroboam thought to himself, *"The kingdom will now likely revert to the house of David. If these people go up to offer sacrifices at the temple of the Lord in Jerusalem, they will again give their allegiance to their lord, Rehoboam king of Judah. They will kill me and return to King Rehoboam."* (Note: when the text reads "go up," it does not mean direction, as in north or south, but rather it refers to the high elevation of Jerusalem.)

He simply did not believe God would do what he promised, and put his own agenda before God's. Solidifying his authority and power were more important to Jeroboam than serving and pleasing God. Holiness took a backseat. Verses 28-30 tell us what he did next. *After seeking advice, the king made two golden calves. He said to the people, "It is too much for you to go up to Jerusalem. Here are your gods, O Israel, who brought you up out of Egypt." One he set up in Bethel, and the other in Dan. And this thing became a sin; the people went even as far as Dan to worship the one there.* He sinned by encouraging God's people to false worship.

There is something more interesting that I want you to glean from this story. God didn't just forget about Jeroboam's sin. In 1 Kings 15:26, we read about his son, Nadab, who took the throne after Jeroboam's death, and of him God said, *He did evil in the eyes of the Lord, walking in the ways of his father and in his sin, which he had caused Israel to commit.* God remembered Jeroboam's sin, and the sin of Israel, because there had been no confession and repentance. In fact, God mentions this man's sin several times in 1 Kings.

- *He* (King Baasha) *did evil in the eyes of the Lord, walking in the ways of _Jeroboam_ and in his sin, which he had caused Israel to commit—*15:34.
- *So he* (Zimri) *died, because of the sins he had committed, doing evil in the eyes of the Lord and walking in the ways of _Jeroboam_ and in the sin he had committed and had caused Israel to commit—*16:18-19.
- *He* (Omri) *walked in all the ways of _Jeroboam_ son of Nebat and in his sin, which he had caused Israel to commit, so that they provoked the Lord, the God of Israel, to anger by their worthless idols –*16:26.
- *He* (Ahab*) not only considered it trivial to commit the sins of _Jeroboam_ son of Nebat, but he also married Jezebel daughter of Ethbaal king of the Sidonians, and began to serve Baal and worship him—*16:31.
- *He* (Ahaziah) *did evil in the eyes of the Lord, because he walked in the ways of his father and mother and in the ways of _Jeroboam_ son of Nebat, who caused Israel to sin—*22:52.

These six passages in 1 Kings show us the sin that needed to be confessed, but wasn't. In 2 Kings we discover that God has not yet "gotten over it," concerning the sin of Jeroboam. God is still remembering the sin, and still waiting for some leader in Israel to not only confess, but to repent, but one king after another continued *walking in the ways of Jeroboam.* Notice that in each passage, God uses the phrase ***did not turn away***.

- *He* (Joram) *got rid of the sacred stone of Baal that his father had made. Nevertheless he clung to the sins of _Jeroboam_ son of Nebat, which he had caused Israel to commit; he **did not turn away** from them—*3:3.
- *He* (Jehu) ***did not turn away*** *from the sins of _Jeroboam_, which he had caused Israel to commit—*10:31.
- *He* (Jehoash) *did evil in the eyes of the Lord and **did not turn away** from any of the sins of _Jeroboam_ son of Nebat, which he had caused Israel to commit; he continued in them—*13:11

- *He (Jeroboam, not the original, but a namesake) did evil in the eyes of the Lord and **did not turn away** from any of the sins of Jeroboam son of Nebat, which he had caused Israel to commit—14:24*
- *He (Zechariah) did evil in the eyes of the Lord, as his fathers had done. He **did not turn away** from the sins of Jeroboam son of Nebat, which he had caused Israel to commit—15:9*
- *He (Menaham) did evil in the eyes of the Lord. During his entire reign he **did not turn away** from the sins of Jeroboam son of Nebat, which he had caused Israel to commit—15:18*
- *Pekehiah did evil in the eyes of the Lord. He **did not turn away** from the sins of Jeroboam son of Nebat, which he had caused Israel to commit—15:24*
- *He (Pekah) did evil in the eyes of the Lord. He **did not turn away** from the sins of Jeroboam son of Nebat, which he had caused Israel to commit—15:28*
- *When he (God) tore Israel away from the house of David, they made Jeroboam son of Nebat their king. Jeroboam enticed Israel away from following the Lord and caused them to commit a great sin. The Israelites persisted in all the sins of Jeroboam and **did not turn away** from them until the Lord removed them from his presence, as he had warned through all his servants the prophets. So the people of Israel were taken from their homeland into exile in Assyria, and they are still there—2 Kings 17:21-23*

I hope you took time to read each of those passages, even though they seem redundant. I want you to recognize that God expects our sin to be dealt with, and he does not simply forget about it or get over it. He does not act as if it never happened, and we shouldn't either! In fact, God mentions this sin of Jeroboam 15 times in these two books, covering 27 chapters. Perhaps more important is to note the amount of time that actually passed: 20 kings, including four not mentioned in these passages, from Jeroboam to Hashea, 208 years! After 208 years God still had Jeroboam's sin on His mind! God was still unhappy about it. God punished the northern kingdom of Israel for following Jeroboam's sin and not turning away from it. That last passage says *the Lord removed them from his presence…!*

Term to Remember: the EXILE was a time in Jewish history when God removed them from the Holy Land and allowed them to be carried into captivity.

Perhaps you are familiar enough with the Bible to know this part of Jewish history. They were taken into captivity, long after their deliverance from Egypt, long after establishing themselves as a nation, after quite a long time in the Promised Land. Perhaps you just never really understood why God did that. It was because they refused to deal with their sin. They refused to confess it and repent, or turn away from it. How could this nation be evangelizing the world, showing them how to have a right relationship with the One True God if their relationship with him was so tainted with sin? They couldn't, so God vomited them out of the Holy Land.

As a Christian, your salvation is not just for your benefit. You are called to be a witness to the lost world around you, and your relationship with him is your greatest tool to witness with. But you must deal with sin on a daily basis. People may be swayed by your verbal testimony, but your holiness will prove your testimony. *If we confess our sins, he is faithful and just and will forgive us our sins and purify us from all unrighteousness. If we claim we have not sinned, we make him out to be a liar and his word has no place in our lives*--1 John 1:9-10. This is the truth about sanctity.

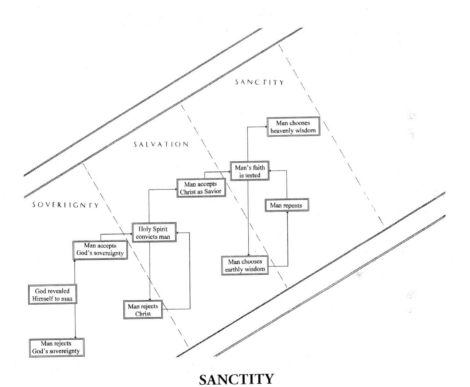

SANCTITY

CHAPTER SEVEN

RENEWING THE MIND

I mentioned in Part Two that holiness for us is easier than for Old Covenant saints, because the law was external but for us it is internal. *I will put my law in their minds and write it on their hearts*--Jeremiah 31:33. There is more to it than that. I believe the Bible teaches that before salvation our minds, under the influence of sin, think in a certain way that is contrary to God. Salvation begins with our cognitive choice to honor what we know about God and seek to know more about Him. Sadly, we know from what we have studied so far that most people reject God and what they know about him. The consequences of sin being introduced into human behavior is that our spirits are dead, our bodies eventually wear out and die, and our minds are bent on rejecting God and his holiness. There is hope, however. Our spirits are resurrected when we accept Christ as our Savior. We are promised a bodily resurrection when we leave this earth. Both of these prove that Christ has conquered death in our spirits and our bodies.

But what about our minds? What about our thought processes? Can our minds really be programmed to think in a way that is more holy, more like God? Or is that just a fantasy? Let's examine some New Testament scriptures, starting with Colossians 1:21--*Once you were alienated from God and were enemies in your minds because of your evil behavior.* Paul wrote this letter to the church at Colosse. It was written to Christians to help them in their understanding of what Christ had really done for them on the cross. It was written to remind them of the state of their minds before they were saved. God loved them enough to send Christ to die for them, but they were enemies of God and his plan before their conversion to Christianity.

You may be thinking to yourself, "I wasn't an enemy of God, even when I was lost!" Well, God says otherwise, and it really is not a stretch at all. If your body is in decay and requires the power of Christ to someday resurrect it, and your spirit was dead and required the power of Christ to resurrect it, what makes you think your mind was somehow untainted by sin? That's just not logical. This state is best described by the theological term **total depravity**. This term is often misunderstood, but simply means that sin affected humans in every aspect of our being. My body was corrupted by sin; my soul was corrupted by sin; my mind was corrupted by sin. All of us, before salvation, were enemies of God in our minds. We thought contrary to God, even if we cognitively chose to look for him and seek him out. It still took the Holy Spirit to initiate salvation in us.

Term to Remember: TOTAL DEPRAVITY means that we cannot claim that any part of our being is untouched by sin. We need God to heal our souls, bodies, and our minds.

I believe that after salvation we still have those memories of when we were enemies of God; that they are written into our minds and still affect the way we think towards God, unless we allow him to renew our minds. You may recall Romans 12: 1-2 from Part Two. It says, *Therefore, I urge you, brothers, in view of God's mercy, to offer your bodies as living sacrifices, holy and pleasing to God—this is your spiritual act of worship. Do not conform any longer to the pattern of this world, but be transformed by the renewing of your mind. Then you will be able to test and approve what God's will is—his good, pleasing and perfect will.*

I have heard it taught that the renewing of your minds is like God erasing the bad stuff and writing the good stuff on your clean chalkboard. That's not really accurate. The Greek word Paul uses here has the connotation of making something new again, rather than just making it clean. He doesn't clean your chalkboard—he gives you a new chalkboard. It means that God wants to renovate your mind from something it used to be to something totally new. He wants to not erase, but eradicate the memories you have of once being his enemy. He doesn't even want to leave a faint shadow of what was once written on your mind. God wants to make your mind new, so you can only think of yourself as his child. God wants to completely change your thought patterns.

You're probably wondering exactly what it means, being an enemy of God in your mind. I believe the answer is found in Romans 8:5-8—*Those who live according to the sinful nature have their minds set on what <u>nature desires</u>; but those who live in accordance with the Spirit have their minds set on what the Spirit desires. The mind of sinful man is <u>death</u>, but the mind controlled by the Spirit is life and peace; the sinful mind is <u>hostile to God</u>. It does not submit to God's law, nor can it do so. Those controlled by the sinful nature <u>cannot please God.</u>*

This passage shows us four ways in which we were enemies of God in our minds when we were lost. I underlined them. First of all, the lost man has his mind set on natural desires, or the desires of the flesh. Some teach that when you are saved your auto-pilot takes over and holiness just happens in you. If that were the case, there would be a lot more holiness in the church! *Be transformed* tells me that I have a responsibility to seek holiness, and so the first thing I need to do is recognize that even as a Christian, I still have some old ways of thinking programmed into my mind. I have not completely abandoned the desires of the flesh.

Here's my point. Let's suppose you are a follower of Christ, trying to live a holy life, trying not to give in to the desires of your flesh. Suddenly you hit one of life's obstacles. You don't understand it, and you get frustrated by it. After all, you are trying to please God. He shouldn't let this happen to you, right? You start to think, "What's the point of trying to be good if God is going to let something like this happen to me? I'm trying to be holy and He's not rewarding me for it! I may as well go back to _____!" You can fill in the blank with whatever you indulged in before you were saved: lusting, lying, cheating, stealing, cursing, gossiping, etc.

Before salvation, you were controlled by the flesh, and God wants to renew your mind, eradicating that way of thinking. He knows that if your mind is not renewed, you will revert back to that way of thinking every time you find yourself struggling in life. You will revert back to your old sins, and become even more discouraged. It is a vicious cycle, one that your loving heavenly Father wants to break.

Let's consider the second point from the passage: the mind of the lost man is on death. You may be thinking, "Ok, I may have struggled with fleshly desires when I was lost, but I was definitely not obsessed with death!" Really? Have you ever said "life stinks!" Or, "life is hard, and then you die!" Maybe you were just joking, but we have all said things like that. When you hit one of life's obstacles, you may have become depressed to the point of thinking about dying. Or you may have gotten so discouraged at times that you asked God to just let you die. I know I have, before God renewed my mind.

Let me stop and say something important. Some depression is clinical, and doctors can determine when and how to treat it. I am not suggesting that all depression is spiritual, but I believe much of it is, simply because the Bible teaches that when we were lost our minds thought of death, and the Bible teaches that God wants our minds made new again. God wants to change the way your mind thinks, so that you think of life, **so that you enjoy life!** He wants to eradicate those memories of death from your mind so you don't go back to them when you face struggles. If mind renewal wasn't necessary, why would he command it? And if it were automatic, why explain all this to us?

Point: God doesn't want us focused on sinful natural desires, death, hostility towards him, or the feeling that we can never please him. He wants to reprogram our minds to think like him.

Let's look at the third point from the passage. He said the mind of the lost man is hostile to God. Perhaps you've had moments in your life when everything is going well and suddenly it all seems to fall apart. If your mind has not been renewed you may go back to your pre-salvation way of thinking. You may think to yourself, "God has let me down again. I'm tired of being disappointed. He's just not going to bless me!" Ever had those thoughts? I have.

How about the fourth point from the scripture, that when you were lost you could not please God? How does that line of thought creep back into our lives? Again, when you face a struggle in life, and your mind has not been renewed, you may think to yourself, "God is punishing me for something. I just can't please him no matter how hard I try. He must be mad at me for some reason!" Ever felt that way? I have.

God does not want you to think of him in those ways. When you think of God as petty, manipulative, disappointing, and depressing, you are assigning him human frailties, which he does not possess. You are treating him like all the people in your life who have hurt you or let you down. You are treating him as if he were a human. You are thinking of yourself as God's enemy, not his child. This is especially difficult if you grew up in a troubled home, if you were abused or neglected as a child. These thought patterns become deeply etched into your mind, and it will take much prayer for you to let God change the way you think. But he can and will do it. God did not hurt you—people did, and God wants you to know he is not another person waiting for the chance to hurt you. He is Almighty God, and he alone can renew your mind and change the way you think.

God doesn't care about just getting your soul saved or issuing you a free pass from hell. He has a plan of redemption and a purpose in that plan for you. He wants you to join him in his work, so naturally he cares about how you think and how that makes you feel. If you don't feel loved by him you will never enjoy his fellowship the way he wants you to. You will never enjoy the mission and the ministry the way you should. If you do serve, it will only be from a sense of obligation. He wants more than that for you. He wants to be your loving Father.

Holiness will come much easier when you let God renew your mind. Now that you know what the scripture teaches about your old way of thinking, you can recognize it when it crosses your mind. Then you can pray about it. You may not feel like praying, but do it anyway. You can be open and honest with God. For example, if you feel like he is not being fair, you can confess to him, reverently, that this is what your mind is thinking. Then you can ask him to tell you the TRUTH. Ask him to change the way your mind thinks, to renew it and give you a mind that thinks like one of his children and not one of his enemies. He will do this for you, because he loves you.

PASSING THE TEST

There is one other point that bears discussing. When God calls us, and we surrender, He may test us to find out if we are sincere. Remember Abraham, from Part One? He was the father of the Jewish people, called by God for a great purpose, but his faith was tested. According to Genesis 12:1, *The Lord had said to Abram, "Leave your country, your people and your father's household and go to the land I will show you."* Abraham was obedient. He surrendered to God's will for his life, packed up and headed out, not even knowing where he was going, but he carried in his heart a great promise from God. *I will make you into a great nation and I will bless you; I will make your name great, and you will be a blessing. I will bless those who bless you, and whoever curses you I will curse; and all people on earth will be blessed through you.* Verses 2-3.

Wow! What an amazing promise and all Abraham had to do to claim the promise was to be obedient and go to the place God would show him. That's it! Just go there, and the blessings will flow! But as soon as obedient Abraham got to the place where God showed him, he faced a test. Verse 10 tells us, *Now there was a famine in the land, and Abram went down to Egypt to live there for a while because the famine was severe.* You may not blame him for leaving right after his arrival, but God did not tell him to go to Egypt. God told him to *go the land I will show you* and *I will bless you.*

Perhaps Abraham was disappointed when he got there and found the living conditions worse than he expected. Perhaps, like us sometimes, he didn't understand, and thought, "What's the point of being obedient if God is going to let something like this happen to me?" If you continue reading Chapter 12 you discover that he reverted back to his <u>natural desires</u>. He lied to the Egyptians about his wife, and asked her to lie as well. He was afraid for his life, even though God had promised to make him into a great nation. How could a dead man with no children become a great nation? Abraham's faith was put to the test and he failed. He reverted back to his old way of thinking. You'll notice he was also thinking about, and worried about, <u>death</u>. Abraham was tested more than once, and he failed more than once, but he kept repenting, and his faith kept growing. He is remembered by the writer of Hebrews as one of the great heroes of faith.

Peter is another man who was tested. Even though Jesus had told him and the other disciples that he must die and rise from the dead, Peter's faith failed him when it all started happening. Peter failed the test. Ultimately, however, Peter repented. His faith grew, and he became one of the primary leaders of the first-century church. He was the one who preached at Pentecost, the day most Christians regard as the birth of the church. We'll discuss Peter's transformation even more in Part Four.

Testing is a good thing. Teachers test students to see what, if anything, they have learned. A good teacher wants to know what you have learned and what areas require more study. Likewise, a loving Father who wants to transform you will test you to see what you have learned and what areas require more study. Count it an honor when your faith is tested. Try very hard not to fail, but if you do, repent and keep going. Anticipate another test. Be ready for it. Don't revert back to your old way of thinking. This is how your faith is developed. It doesn't come from just saying one prayer or just desiring to have faith. It comes from working your faith. Trust what you have learned about your Father. Trust His love.

KNOWING GOD'S WILL

So what is the point of pursuing holiness and transformation? Well, obviously, it pleases God, and after all he has done for mankind, it is not really that much to ask of us. It strengthens our relationship with him, helping us feel his love. There is another point, however. Seeking holiness and allowing God to transform us allows him to use us in his plan. It's all about knowing God's will and every Christian asks at some point in his life, "what is God's will for me?" So, how can you know his will for your life, what he has called you to do? In my church I have taught this and called it "Becoming a Level Four Christian." Let me explain. We know from scripture three different aspects of God's will that are spelled out for us very clearly.

1. We know from scripture that God's will for all humans is <u>salvation</u>. 2 Peter 3:9 says, *The Lord is not slow in keeping his promise, as some understand slowness. He is patient with you, not wanting anyone to perish, but everyone to come to repentance.*

2. We also know from scripture that God's will for those who accept salvation is <u>holiness</u>. 1 Thessalonians 4:7 says, *For God did not call us to be impure, but to live a holy life.* Once your salvation is secure, God isn't finished working in your life. He wants you to pursue holiness.

3. We know from scripture that God's will for those who seek holiness is <u>transformation</u>. The first part of Romans 12:2 tells us, *Do not conform any longer to the pattern of this world, but be transformed by the renewing of your mind.* God realizes that holiness is difficult to achieve in this sinful world. That's why he offers to transform us by renewing our minds. It's important for you to realize that God doesn't call you to be saved, demand holiness, and then say "Good luck!" He has a plan to make it happen for us, if we allow it.

4. We then know from scripture that God does want to reveal to you his will for your life. The second part of Romans 12:2 says, *Then you will be able to test and approve what God's will is—his good, pleasing and perfect will.* I'm glad God didn't call me to the ministry when I was a teenager, because I knew so little about sanctity—confession, repentance, transformation. Even when he did reveal his will for me, calling me to the ministry, He spent the first couple of years just leading me to understand sanctity, before he gave me a place to serve. And even then, he did not call me to be a pastor until I had been in the transformation process for ten years! I was forty when God finally revealed to me *his good, pleasing and perfect will* for my life.

I am convinced that most Christians have never been taught the principles of holiness and transformation--they've never been taught the truth about sanctity. Instead, most never make it to level four, knowing God's will for their lives. You simply cannot move from level one to level four and skip levels two and three. If you are a Christian, but are not seeking holiness, then you are not doing God's will. This is not his mysterious will, but his clearly-stated will found in the Bible. If you are not going through a transformation process, then you are not doing God's will. It is clearly stated in the scripture that this is what he wants you to do. So, why would God tell you more about his will for you if you are not doing what he has already told you? He won't.

If you are a Christian, then you have completed the first level, but you are far from done. If you are a Christian, then you know, according to God's word, that his will for you is to be holy. You also know that his will for you is to be transformed. Then, and only then, can you begin to really know what h*is good, pleasing and perfect will* is for the rest of your life. This is the truth about sanctity.

PART THREE REVIEW

Terms to Remember:

SANCTITY—holiness

CONFESSION—admitting when we are wrong

REPENTANCE—turning away from the wrong behavior

RECONCILIATION—making things harmonious again

EXILE—the time that God's people were vomited out of the Holy Land because they refused the call to holiness, confession, repentance, and reconciliation

TOTAL DEPRAVITY—my mind, body and soul all need to be affected by God's redemption

---

Points:
- **WE DON'T LIKE TO ADMIT WHEN WE'RE WRONG**
- **GOD WANTS TO REPROGRAM OUR MINDS**

PART FOUR

THE
TRUTH
ABOUT
STEWARDSHIP

CHAPTER EIGHT

MORE THAN MONEY

One of my pastors once preached a very rousing sermon on stewardship. It was almost an hour of why we should give ten percent of our income to the church. He claimed that if you gave ten percent of your income, God would so bless your finances that you would be able to do more with the ninety percent that was left over than you could ever do with one hundred percent. He claimed that we would never be in need. In fact, he was so sure of his belief that he challenged our church to try it for one year. He said that if anyone in the congregation that day was not a tither, but would commit to tithing for one year, he would personally guarantee the results. He offered to refund all the money they gave over that year if, at year's end, they were unhappy with the results. He wasn't quite clear about whether the refund would come from the church coffers or his own personal savings! But he was adamant that anyone who took the challenge would be amazed at how much more money they would have.

Apparently, no one accepted the challenge, because there was no noticeable increase in giving that year. In fact, the church was forced to shrink its budget the next year, because we were struggling to make ends meet. Many church members complained about the staff and how much they were paid, though it was actually on the low end of the scale for comparable churches. At the same time, however, the members were totally dependent on the staff to carry out the work of the church. They often said to the pastor and other ministerial staff, "You can do that yourself! That's what we pay you for!" That was a very hard-working staff. Getting church members to commit to ministry was often difficult, and getting them to actually show up was sometimes even more difficult. We were missing the **truth about stewardship**.

Term to Remember: STEWARDSHIP means taking care of something important.

So, if you think this section is about tithing and money, you are only partially correct, and mostly wrong. I am a firm believer in tithing, and personally give a little more than ten percent of my income. I have never, however, preached a sermon on tithing. That may shock you, but it's true. What may shock you even more is that every year I have served my congregation, giving has increased. I have preached stewardship, but that entails much more than money.

A steward is properly defined as someone entrusted with managing the money, property, or affairs of someone else. As Christians, most of us have been taught that the money we earn is not really our own but God's, and we are merely stewards of it. This is true, but that is only a portion of the truth about stewardship. We have been entrusted with managing the money, property, and affairs of God's church. Stewardship means caring for something that is worth caring for. In other words—something valuable. I don't think we can understand the truth about stewardship until we understand the value of the church.

Hopefully by now you have a greater understanding of "the big picture," God's great plan of redemption. In Part One I attempted to explain the sovereignty of God Almighty—that he is just that—Almighty. He is the only Creator. He created on a scale that would demand our attention. He has revealed more and more about himself to us over the course of human history. The height of that revelation was his own Son, Jesus Christ, taking on human flesh to show us exactly Who God is. He has even intervened in human history in an effort to coax us into seeking him out. He reigns over us whether or not we want it or accept it. It is the fact and the truth of God's sovereignty.

In Part Two, we learned how salvation starts and where it leads. It begins with our acknowledging what we already know about God. At a minimum, according to scripture, we all know certain things about God. He exists. He is eternal, having always existed. His power is eternal, meaning He did not evolve from a lower being. He is divine, meaning that he is perfect and holy. Our seeking him involves acknowledging these fundamental truths about him, giving him the honor and gratitude he deserves. He sends his Holy Spirit to convict us of our sinfulness and show us the glory of Jesus Christ. Accepting Christ as our Savior allows God's Spirit to dwell in our souls and starts us on a path of spiritual growth and maturity. This is the truth of salvation.

In Part Three, I explained the need for sanctification in our lives. It is the process by which God changes us from the inside out, renewing our minds, and transforming us to be more like Christ. God wants you and me to know beyond any shadow of doubt that we are his children and that he is our loving Father. He gives us direction, especially through the work of his Holy Spirit. He sometimes tests us to see if we are growing and developing our faith. He reveals more of his will for us, even the specific ways he wants to use each of us in his ministry, the church. This is the truth about sanctity.

In Part Five, we will examine the difference between God's true, loyal leaders, and those who are false. God has harsh words for those who would lead Christians astray, and for those who make no real attempt to teach the truths about God. It is ignorance that causes God's people to wander around in the fog, and God wants true pastors, shepherds, who will care for His people, encourage them, educate them, and expect them to grow and mature. This is the truth about shepherds.

Here you find the basic foundational truths of the church. The church must recognize God and worship him and him only, because he is **sovereign**. The church must believe in and share the gospel of Jesus Christ, because it is our only **salvation**. The church must grow up spiritually, seeking holiness and transformation, because **sanctity** keeps us in fellowship with God. The church must raise up great leaders whom God can use to perpetuate the spreading of the gospel, because we need **shepherds** to keep us out of the fog. The church is the institution God has created and chosen to carry out his redemptive work in this dispensation.

Thus it is often called The Church Age, and we are called to be good stewards of his church.

- -

GOD IS SOVEREIGN
HE ALONE OFFERS SALVATION
HE THEN CALLS US TO SANCTITY
HE GIVES US SHEPHERDS TO LEAD US

- -

And yet, so many Christians neglect the church. Many members are only spectators, watching ministry happen but not actually participating. Many expect the ministerial staff to do all the work. After all, that is their job, right? We will never be proper stewards of the church until we know its value. To know the value God places on the church, it helps to go to God's word, the Bible, to see what God says about it. Revelation 19:7-8 give us a glimpse into the future, a time when the church has been taken to heaven. God speaks of the church as the bride of Christ. *Let us rejoice and be glad and give him glory! For the wedding of the Lamb has come, and his bride has made herself ready. Fine linen, bright and clean, was given her to wear.* It has no sexual or romantic connotation. Rather, it rejoices in the coming day when the church age is over and we, the church, can enjoy complete and intimate fellowship with our Savior, Jesus Christ.

We do not have to wait, however, to enjoy this wonderful relationship with our Savior. Ephesians 5: 31-32 tell us, *"For this reason a man will leave his father and mother and be united to his wife, and the two will become one flesh." This is a profound mystery—but I am talking about Christ and the church.* Paul is teaching that the church is bound to Jesus just like a husband and wife. We are one with Christ! Like it or not, if you are a Christian, you are inescapably bound to the rest of His church! You are one part of a body, and you cannot function properly on your own.

Romans 12:4-5 tell us, *Just as each of us has one body with many members, and these members do not all have the same function, so in Christ we who are many form one body, and each member belongs to all the others.* I have heard many people say over the years, "I don't have to go to church to be a Christian." That is true. Church attendance doesn't provide salvation.

But this completely misses the point. Church is not a building; it is a living organism, a body. Each Christian is a part of this body. Church is not someplace you visit—it is something you are. We must distinguish between "going to church" and being the church. If you are a Christian who doesn't "go to church" you are like a part of the body that refuses to serve its function.

The next few verses, 6-8, explain: *We have different gifts, according to the grace given us. If a man's gift is prophesying, let him use it in proportion to his faith. If it is serving, let him serve; if it is teaching, let him teach; if it is encouraging, let him encourage; if it is contributing to the needs of others, let him give generously; if it is leadership, let him govern diligently; if it is showing mercy, let him do it cheerfully.* Staying at home is not listed as one of your possible gifts.

Hopefully, just knowing that we, the church, are the bride of Christ would be enough to encourage you to get involved. Knowing that you are part of the body of Christ should motivate you. If Jesus Christ regards the church highly enough to be united with it, shouldn't you? Are your standards higher than his? No, they are not.

Consider Paul's letter to the church at Ephesus, recorded in Ephesians 5:25-30. *Husbands, love your wives, just as Christ loved the church and gave himself up for her to make her holy, cleansing her by the washing with water through the word, and to present her to himself as a radiant church, without stain or wrinkle or any other blemish, but holy and blameless.* If you are a Christian, you need to stop and ponder the fact that Jesus Christ died for the church, *to make her holy!* Of course, holiness is a personal thing—it starts with you and me—but holiness is also a corporate thing. And we have been called as stewards of the church, to take care of it and nurture it, to aid in the maturation and holiness process. Stewardship is about much more than just giving your tithes and offerings. Stewardship involves four different processes in the life of the church. I call them the Four Corners of Stewardship and they are: Evangelism, Discipline, Discipleship, and Priorities. When we talk about being good stewards, we are talking about supporting the church. Like the corners of a building that support the structure above, these four corners of stewardship are the support processes of the church. When we fail in one corner, it produces stress on the others. They are all vital.

MY LESSON IN STEWARDSHIP

Before we go any further, however, I need to tell you why I place evangelism first on that list. I need to tell you the rest of the story. Before God made me the Minister of Music, Education, and Outreach at FBC I was just a member, but God had a plan for my life. I knew he was calling me to serve that church, and there was no one to lead our music ministry. I had filled in for our worship leader in the past, and many in the church were affirming that perhaps God had placed me there for a reason. There was some opposition, however. I was offered a lay position in the church, Sunday School Director, and though I didn't feel convicted to fill that position, I did agree to pray about it. I felt convicted by God to fast for two days, and so I did. On the afternoon of the second day, God confirmed that he was not calling me to be the Sunday School Director. He had other plans for me. He gave me a vision for our church.

I was a member of our Church Growth and Development Committee, which had been chartered to find a vision for our congregation's future, and find solutions to our problems. Our sanctuary was bursting at the seams because it only held about 250, so we were seating worshipers in the lobby watching the service on a screen. Not exactly optimal. Some Sundays people would enter and leave for lack of seating. We had a large open room in another building, what we called the Christian Life Center, or CLC, essentially a basketball court, that was seldom used except for Easter services and revivals, when the sanctuary and lobby proved utterly incapable of handling the crowds. At the same time, our Sunday School space was underused because that ministry had not been nurtured. Many rooms were unused or mispurposed.

When God spoke to me that second day of fasting, I immediately went to my truck, grabbed a pad and pen, and began to write. I wrote at the top of the page "Priorities" and then listed them, under his conviction: Worship, Education, and Recreation. The very first thing God wanted to talk to me about was worship. We were reserving a basketball court that was rarely used, and yet we were turning people away who came to worship the Almighty God. That was a shameful lack of stewardship. We needed to repurpose that big empty room and use it for worship. The existing sanctuary would make an ideal multi-purpose space for fellowships and classrooms. We wouldn't be able to play ball in the church, but we would be able to accommodate 500 or more in worship without building a new structure, and the CLC was desperately in need of an overhaul anyway.

The second priority for us was education, and that was an area we admittedly had neglected. When I later became a staff member, I explained to the church that no matter how large our sanctuary was, we would never likely grow beyond the limits we placed on Sunday School. The Sunday School ministry is where we make disciples. It's where we mentor new leaders, bring in the lost and teach them about Christ in a small group setting, and how we build long-term relationships in the church body. We were attracting many more people to worship than Sunday School, which meant that many were participators only, not getting involved in the work of the church. Again, that is not a good example of stewardship. By repurposing some of our educational space, and making the sanctuary a multi-purpose space, we would be able to accommodate 500 in Sunday School, as opposed to the 250 we currently handled.

God convicted me that our church had designated more space and resources for recreation than practically anything else. While fellowship is important, it did not deserve first place, but third. The worship and wonder of our God was to be first in our hearts. The teaching and discipling of God's children was to be second. Recreation and fellowship among God's people was the final part of a well-rounded congregation. Even though our church was attracting visitors and seeing some growth, we were not healthy. In fact, we were quite dysfunctional, but God gave us a vision for fixing that. He gave us a vision for using our space to accommodate more people, and to eventually build more space for even more people. God was calling us to **evangelism**! He was getting our priorities in line, getting our hearts in line, and preparing us for the people he would send to us.

Now, here's where it gets interesting. Remember that I told you at the beginning of this chapter that our church was struggling financially? The year God gave me his vision was the year our budget had been downsized in an effort to get our finances in order. The pastor's challenge on tithing had not rendered much effect on the budget situation. So naturally, when I presented the vision to my fellow committee members, there was concern about how we would pay for renovations. God had given me the vision in three phases. Phase One was simple and would only cost $4000. Phase

Two, however, involved renovating the CLC and the education building, and even with our own people providing most of the labor, would cost $125,000. I didn't make up these numbers. God literally gave them to me, and they turned out to be very accurate.

Let me give you a timeline. God gave me this vision in late August of 2006. Our church had just borrowed $10,000 from our building fund to pay bills. I presented the three-phase plan to the committee in September, and we spent the winter months discussing and planning, and actually implementing much of Phase One. It didn't require a church vote, and one of our committee members donated the funds for it. We presented the entire plan to the church in February, and it barely passed, literally by 51%. Giving up the basketball court proved to be a huge hurdle! In April, we voted to spend the first $65,000 of Phase Two. This would renovate our CLC and turn it into a temporary worship space. By this time, in April, our church finances had improved so dramatically that we had been running a surplus every month since September, the month I first submitted this vision. In fact, in April we had well over $65,000 in the general fund, so the church would have no need to raise or borrow money. God had already provided the money! That vote was nearly unanimous, with only one dissenter. He was hard of hearing and didn't understand that the church had the money on hand. Afterward, someone explained this to him and he offered to rescind his "no" vote. He just didn't want the church going into debt. I don't blame him.

By this time God had convinced me that if our church would be obedient to his vision, he would make it happen. We did renovate the CLC and move our worship services into that new space. No more crowding. No more turning people away. We ordered 500 chairs and the first Sunday in that building most of those seats were occupied by worshipers. It gets even better, though. Even as we spent the $65,000 on that project, by the time it was finished we had even more than that in our general fund. Our budget started to resemble the widow's oil in 1 Kings 17. No matter how much we poured out for God's plan, it never ran out, but multiplied. So we spent another $65,000 to renovate our educational space, bringing the total Phase 2 cost to exactly what God had told me: $125,000. And guess what, after all that spending, we **still** had about $140,000 in our general fund, and our building fund had doubled. More importantly, we now had the space to accommodate 500 in worship and 500 in Sunday School. Phases One and Two were complete, and God had proven that he could indeed make Phase Three happen.

God was trying to teach our church those four corners of stewardship: Evangelism, Discipline, Discipleship, and Priorities. God had given me this vision in August of 2006, and at our Thanksgiving banquet of 2008, I presented the details for Phase Three, including plans for a new permanent sanctuary and more educational space. The church loved it. A lot had happened in that two years and three months. Our pastor had resigned to take another position. I became Minister of Music, Education, and Outreach, and we voted to hire a new pastor. At Thanksgiving, the church was applauding what God was doing. We were united. We finally had a vision for our future, a plan that was working, and our people were motivated. Three months later the pastor fired me, left the church and took about half the congregation with him.

That's when God told me to write this book. It is not enough for God's people to simply know they are saved. Of course that's critical to each of us, but we must know the truth about God's sovereignty. We must know the truth about salvation. We must know the truth about sanctity. And yes, we absolutely must know the truth about shepherds. When we know these truths, we can know the true value of the church. When we know how valuable it is we can be good stewards of it.

CHAPTER NINE

STEWARDSHIP IS EVANGELISM

The church is not a static institution. It is a more like a living, breathing organism. That's why Paul referred to the church as *a body*. It is not a body, however, that has reached its growth potential and stopped growing; at least it shouldn't have stopped growing. If you recall what we covered in Part One, this is the Church Age, or the Age of Grace. This is the time God has appointed to bring salvation to all corners of the earth. We talked earlier about God's patience, from 2 Peter 3:9, where we learn that God is being patient because He is *not wanting anyone to perish, but everyone to come to repentance.* This is the age to preach Jesus. This is the age of evangelism.

Term to Remember: EVANGELISM is the spreading of the gospel message of Jesus Christ.

If you are not actively involved in evangelism, then you are not fulfilling the purpose of the church. That means you are not fulfilling your purpose. In Luke 16:19-31, Jesus' own words are recorded as he told the story of the rich man and Lazarus. Maybe you are familiar with this story, though you probably never associated it with stewardship. Paint an image in your mind as you read verses 19-21. *There was a rich man who was dressed in purple and fine linen and lived in luxury every day. At his gate was laid a beggar named Lazarus, covered with sores and longing to eat what fell from the rich man's table. Even the dogs came and licked his sores.*

This is a sad story, because even the toughest among us feel our hearts melt at the idea of someone suffering and hungry. The situation changes however, quite dramatically, upon the death of these two men. Verses 22-24 explain. *The time came when the beggar died and the angels carried him to Abraham's side. The rich man also died and was buried. In hell, where he was in torment, he looked up and saw Abraham far away, with Lazarus by his side. So he called to him, "Father Abraham, have pity on me and send Lazarus to dip the tip of his finger in water and cool my tongue, because I am in agony in this fire.*

Let me stop and explain the scenario. The word that is rendered "hell" is the Greek word "hades." Most theologians believe that before Christ's resurrection and return to heaven, all those who died under the old covenant went to Hades. There were, according to what Jesus said here in this passage, two sections: one for the righteous, referred to as "Abraham's bosom," and another for the unrighteous. However, it is generally assumed that when Jesus resurrected and returned to heaven he took the righteous in Hades with him to heaven. Ephesians 4:8-9 may allude to this. *This is why it says: "When he ascended on high, he led captives in his train and gave gifts to men." What does "he ascended" mean except that he also descended to the lower, earthly regions?*

According to Paul's teaching in 2 Corinthians 5:8, the saved today go immediately to heaven: *We are confident, I say, and would prefer to be away from the body and at home with the Lord.* Scripture tells us that Jesus reigns in heaven, *at the right hand of God,* Acts 7:55. Now, back to the story.

The rich man in Hades was suffering terribly. Lazarus, in life, would have been content just to eat what fell from the rich man's table. Now, after death, he is completely satisfied. The rich man, on the other hand, implies that he would be content with just one drop of water to cool his tongue. Consider verses 25-26: *But Abraham replied, "Son, remember that in your lifetime you received your good things, while Lazarus received bad things, but now he is comforted here and you are in agony. And besides all this, between us and you a great chasm has been fixed, so that those who want to go from here to you cannot, nor can anyone cross over from there to us."*

We know the rich man was Jewish, because he referred to Abraham as "Father Abraham," and Abraham referred to him as "Son." As a Jew, he should have understood God's purpose for Israel on this earth, that they were called to show the world what it means to have a proper relationship with the One True God. This required stewardship, and this rich man was obviously unwilling to share his wealth even for a righteous, hungry man at his gate. But there is so much more to this story.

Abraham explained to him that there was a great chasm fixed between them. We assume, of course, that those on the punishment side of Hades would certainly cross over to the paradise side if given the chance. But did you notice what Abraham said about that chasm working both ways? He said it existed *so that those who want to go from here to you cannot.* It is almost impossible to fathom, but apparently there were those in Abraham's bosom who would, if allowed, cross over into the realm of agony to reach their lost brothers, even if just to offer a fingertip full of water! Perhaps Lazarus was one of those people. Perhaps he would have left his comfort to cross over into the flames, for the sake of another. God had to establish a barrier to keep that from happening.

Amazing, isn't it? Do you know anyone who has such a heart for evangelism? Do we value others above our own comfort? We talk about getting out of our comfort zone, but for most of us it is just talk. When we try to make necessary changes in the church, like giving up basketball for worship, some people will revolt. They vote "NO!"

There is more to the story of the rich man. Verses 27-31 tell us a lot about evangelism. *He answered, "Then I beg you, father, send Lazarus to my father's house, for I have five brothers. Let him warn them, so that they will not also come to this place of torment." Abraham replied,"They have Moses and the Prophets; let them listen to them." "No, father Abraham," he said, "but if someone from the dead goes to them, they will repent." He said to him, "If they do not listen to Moses and the Prophets, they will not be convinced even if someone rises from the dead."*

What was Jesus teaching us in this story? I believe Jesus was offering us a lesson in personal stewardship, the proper use of our money, for example, but it seems evangelism is the greater lesson here. This rich man was apparently not concerned about the things of God. He was not interested in doing God's will or being part of God's plan. If he had, he would not have ended up in the torment side of Hades. He was "lost," as we call it today. Since he wasn't concerned about his relationship with God and his future, he apparently wasn't concerned about his brothers' relationship with God and their future, until it was too late. Evangelism is the first process of stewardship.

Abraham was absolutely right to say that the rich man and his brothers had Moses and the Prophets to listen to. That means they had God's written revelation, the Old Testament, to teach them what they needed to know to have a right relationship with God under the old covenant. But what about today? Under the new covenant, we have the New Testament, the final and full revelation of Jesus Christ. It is everything we need to find salvation. Still, many will not listen. That's why God did something different in the Church Age. He sent the Holy Spirit to convict the world. In John 16:8-11 Jesus said, *"When he comes, he will convict the world of guilt in regard to sin and righteousness and judgment: in regard to sin, because men do not believe in me; in regard to righteousness, because I am going to the Father, where you can see me no longer; and in regard to judgment, because the prince of this world (Satan) now stands condemned."*

In other words, Jesus taught us that we would not only have the testimony of God's Word, including his gospel message, but we would also have the convicting power of the Holy Spirit working on the earth to aid in our evangelism. The Holy Spirit is convicting the lost world about sin, particularly the sin of rejecting Christ. He is convicting the world about righteousness, and the fact that death will come to all of us, and we will either go the Father, as Jesus did, or go to the place of torment, as did the rich man in the story. He is convicting the world about judgment, because those who follow the world's ways, as opposed to God's ways, will be judged, just like Satan has been. Jesus said that the Holy Spirit is convicting the world of sin, death, and hell.

That's why we must, as a church, depend on the Spirit of God to go before us in our outreach and evangelism. All the cards, visits, and phone calls will be ineffective unless there is conviction. We can call on God to convict the people of our community. We can ask God to make our evangelism effective. That's what the Holy Spirit was sent here to do! Why don't we pray more for the lost? But just as importantly, we must be proper stewards of God's church. When we function properly, under the guidance and direction of the Holy Spirit, it will manifest itself in the church. The community will notice. Hebrews 2:3-4 explains. *This salvation, which was first announced by the Lord, was confirmed to us by those who heard him. God also testified to it by signs, wonders and various miracles, and gifts of the Holy Spirit distributed according to his will.*

What does this mean? Quite simply, it means that when Jesus came to usher in the new covenant and announce salvation, God the Father confirmed it by *signs, wonders and various miracles* performed by Jesus. But the *gifts of the Holy Spirit distributed according to his will* would be the spiritual gifts given to the church. We talked about those gifts of the Holy Spirit in the last chapter, from Romans 12:6-8. *We have different gifts, according to the grace given us. If a man's gift is prophesying, let him use it in proportion to his faith. If it is serving, let him serve; if it is teaching, let him teach; if it is encouraging, let him encourage; if it is contributing to the needs of others, let him give generously; if it is leadership, let him govern diligently; if it is showing mercy, let him do it cheerfully.*

That means that the church, by using its spiritual gifts, is testifying to the truth of the gospel message. If we do not allow those spiritual gifts to be used in the church, our testimony becomes weak and ineffective. That's why stewardship matters so much. When we know the truth of God's sovereignty, salvation, sanctity, and shepherds, we can know how to function as the church—how to be good stewards of it. Only then can the Holy Spirit truly manifest himself in the church, and only then can we do what he has called us to do: evangelize the world.

CHAPTER TEN

STEWARDSHIP IS DISCIPLINE

If the first corner of stewardship is evangelism, and growing the church, then the second must be discipline, maintaining the integrity of the church. Many congregations will try almost any approach to grow their numbers, and the world stands ready to offer its suggestions. Therein lies one of the chief conflicts within the church: heavenly wisdom vs. earthly wisdom. Heavenly wisdom springs from the desire to do things God's way, not man's way; to please God and follow his desires regardless of the human consequences. How do we develop heavenly wisdom? Obviously, studying God's Word is the beginning. A strong prayer life is critical. But from a more philosophical point of view, it is simply knowing the truths about God and his sovereignty and applying those truths to your decision-making process. Psalm 111:10 says, *The fear of the Lord is the beginning of wisdom; all who follow his precepts have good understanding. To him belongs eternal praise.*

Term to Remember: DISCIPLINE means that we, the church, make up our minds to always seek God's wisdom as we care for His church. We should never resort to using earthly wisdom.

A precept is simply a rule or standard, so following God's precepts means following his rules and living by his standards. This helps us have understanding. Heavenly wisdom does not come to those who follow the rules and standards of the world. They may develop earthly wisdom, but which would you rather have: wisdom from below or wisdom from above? The church is a heavenly institution that functions on the earth. In fact, the church is the ONLY heavenly institution functioning on the earth. It is not an earthly institution and should never accept earthly wisdom as a substitute for heavenly wisdom. The church was ordained by the Father in heaven and is ruled by Christ from heaven. The Holy Spirit was sent from heaven to direct the affairs of the church. As such, the church should never, ever bow down to any earthly institution, no matter how great or impressive it may seem.

One glaring example is our abuse of education. I certainly believe in education. In fact, the entire point of this book is to educate the church on biblical truths. But the church has, in recent decades, placed so much emphasis on the earthly education of their pastors that their heavenly education has suffered. Seminaries can be wonderful places for ministers to learn, but the seminary is still an earthly institution, and the church would do well to remember that. A certain level of earthly education is critical to even be considered for service at most congregations today, but how do we quantify an anointing? In most cases, we don't even try. We have largely replaced an anointing of God with a diploma. It is purely anecdotal, but it appears to me that we have more PhD's behind the pulpit than ever before in the history of the American church, and yet we are largely ineffective at spreading the gospel in this nation. Wisdom and understanding are scarce. We are losing ground quickly.

I love what Jeremiah said. *But God made the earth by his _power_; he founded the world by his _wisdom_ and stretched out the heavens by his _understanding_,* Jeremiah 10:12. Think about what we learned in Part One about God's sovereignty. He created the "house" as we called it. The universe and all it contains was created by him by his power. (General Revelation) It is magnificent in scale and majesty, designed to impress us and warrant our attention. Only God has the power to do that. He is the only Builder. We often rely on our own power to solve our problems and make our decisions, but our power is very limited and very small compared to God's. In fact, what little power we do have is what God bestowed on us. He is the source of power, so why not go directly to the source? It seems logical, and yet we seldom do it. *God made the earth by his power.* He can handle our problems.

We also learned that God did not just create us, put us on this planet and say, "Good luck!" He has orchestrated human history so that we might look for him and find him. He created humanity in two genders, established the marriage and home (1ˢᵗ Dispensation), made us morally responsible (2ⁿᵈ Dispensation), established human government (3ʳᵈ Dispensation), and gave us moral and civil laws to live by (5ᵗʰ Dispensation). In other words, *he founded the world by his wisdom.* What we call human civilization was actually God's idea, his plan all along. He established the world and its governing laws—they are his precepts that lead us to understanding. Humans did not invent these things. They came from a very wise God. He is the source of all wisdom, so why not go directly to the source? He can make wise decisions for us.

God has also created and maintained a timeline for human history. We can study the dispensations and know what point of that timeline we are on. We are in the Church Age. Every age or dispensation before this one was ordained and implemented by God. He exists outside of time—he created time for our sake, and he is the great Timekeeper. The heavens are being *stretched out* with the passing of time. Science knows that the universe had a point of origin because the universe is expanding. It is being *stretched out.* We measure time by minutes, hours, days, years, etc. but God is not so limited. The marching of time can be measured on God's scale by the expansion of the heavens, and God himself is in control of that process! That means he understands all of human history, everything that has happened and everything that will happen. He promised to send Christ into the world (4ᵗʰ Dispensation), and at just the appropriate time he did it, ushering in the Church Age (6ᵗʰ Dispensation). Nothing surprises him and nothing ever will. He alone has control over time and events. You may not understand what is happening in your life right now, but he does. He can be trusted.

King Jehoshaphat is a good example of someone who understood God's power, wisdom and understanding. You may recall from Part Three on sanctity our discussion of Jeroboam, the first king of the northern kingdom, after Israel split. Jehoshaphat was the fourth king of the southern kingdom, called Judah. His story is recorded in 2 Chronicles. In Chapter

20, Jehoshaphat is informed that a very large army is headed toward Judah. It is, in fact, a coalition army from three different nations, headed his way with destruction on their agenda. Verse 3 reveals his reaction. *Alarmed, Jehoshaphat resolved to inquire of the Lord, and he proclaimed a fast for all Judah. The people of Judah came together to seek help from the Lord; indeed, they came from every town in Judah to seek him.*

The king's first reaction was to inquire of the Lord. As Christians, and as members of God's church, that should always be our first reaction. Unfortunately, we often figure out what we want to do and then pray, asking God to bless our plans. I have sat in committee meetings, as a church member, where prayer only came at the end, after the decision-making process was over. That is backwards. Jehoshaphat was resolute in putting God first. That's great leadership. He then addressed the people who had assembled at the temple, seeking God.

The first thing Jehoshaphat did was appeal to God's power. He said, according to verses 5-6, *"O Lord, God of our fathers, are you not the God who is in heaven? You rule over all the kingdoms of the nations. Power and might are in your hand, and no one can withstand you."* He understood that the God who *made the earth by his power* not only ruled over Judah, who accepted him, but was also ruler over Judah's enemies, whether or not they accepted or acknowledged him. God is sovereign!

Jehoshaphat then appealed to God's wisdom, recognizing that the very existence of the Jewish people was ordained by God as part of his plan of redemption. God had driven out the wicked people of that land and declared it a holy land and planted his people there as his first evangelists to the world. Verses 7-8 record more of the king's prayer. *"O our God, did you not drive out the inhabitants of this land before your people Israel and give it forever to the descendants of Abraham your friend? They have lived in it and have built in it a sanctuary for your Name..."* (Note: When he uses the name Israel, he is not referring to the northern kingdom where Jeroboam reigns, but to the Jewish people as a whole, as they were united when they first occupied the holy land.)

Jehoshaphat then appealed to God's understanding. *"But now here are men from Ammon, Moab and Mount Seir, whose territory you would not allow Israel to invade when they came from Egypt; so they turned away from them and did not destroy them. See how they are repaying us by coming to drive us out of the possession you gave us as an inheritance."* When Israel was going into the Promised Land, God told them not to bother these nations who are now attacking. Apparently, God did not consider them a threat to his new nation and his plan of redemption, so he left them alone. You can understand why Jehoshaphat is now confused that these people who God spared are now approaching with a vast army to destroy him and God's people.

It's okay to admit that you don't understand what's happening around you. Jehoshaphat was perplexed by the situation facing Judah. But he never tried to handle it himself. He turned to God. He resolved to inquire of the Lord. He prayed to God, calling on his power, his wisdom, and his understanding. He feared the Lord, and that is the beginning of wisdom. He followed God's precepts, and that brings understanding. The last sentence of verse 12 sums up the heart of this king when he said to God, *We do not know what to do, but our eyes are upon you.*

If you read the remainder of 2 Chronicles 20 you discover that God spoke to the assembly, through someone with the gift of prophecy. God assured their safety, recorded in verse 15, *This is what the Lord says to you: "Do not be afraid of this vast army. For the battle is not yours, but God's."* This coalition army never had a chance to destroy Judah, because God didn't allow them to. He did allow them to attack each other and destroy themselves.

Living through faith is easier said than done. You may recall from Part Three on sanctity our discussion about renewal of the mind. I shared with you four ways that the Bible says we thought about God when we were lost, and that as Christians those thought patterns still exist and have to be surrendered to God. Through prayer, God can and will change the way we think, so that when trouble arises, we remember first that we are God's children. It is far easier to trust God when your mind considers him a loving Father, as opposed to an enemy. Jehoshaphat's situation could have caused him to doubt God, to doubt his position as a child of God. Thankfully he didn't think that way. He appealed directly to his Father in heaven, who is the source of all power, wisdom, and understanding.

There is a greater point, however. When we rely on our own power, wisdom, and understanding, instead of God's, we are offering ourselves as a substitute for God. An idol is just that—a substitute for the One True

God. You may not say it out loud, or even admit it in your mind, but when you choose to trust your judgment over God's you have idolized yourself. Christians do this all the time. I preached a sermon once titled, "What You Believe Doesn't Matter." I was explaining that if our belief system comes from the world it won't match God's, and therefore it doesn't matter. I have heard statements like, "I know that the Bible says _____, but I just believe _____." A man I once knew told me that God had given him permission to divorce his wife because he had fallen in love with another woman. He had committed adultery, which is clearly a sin according to God's word, and he had absolutely no Biblical grounds to divorce his wife. **God did not tell him to get a divorce**. He believed it was okay and edited the Bible to fit his desires. He was acting as his own god.

I once knew a pastor search committee who felt God was calling a certain man to pastor their church, but the committee chairman said, "We decided that we needed someone with more experience." He didn't even realize what he was admitting to: that his committee had overruled God. They had made their choice, even in disobedience, and then had the nerve to pray and ask God to bless their decision! Why would you ask God to bless your idolatry!

Maintaining the integrity of the church requires leaders like Jehoshaphat, who will lead their people to inquire of the Lord first. True shepherds will remind the church that the God we worship is powerful, wise and understanding, and that there is no worthy substitute, least of all us.

CHAPTER ELEVEN

STEWARDSHIP IS DISCIPLESHIP

Once we understand the absolute necessity of evangelism, growing the church, we must be careful to maintain the integrity of the church through discipline. We create a safe environment for winning the lost to Christ and teach them to trust in the power, wisdom and understanding of God. The next step is making disciples of them and training them to be leaders of God's church. We must teach them how to use their gifts to perpetuate the ministry of the church. This is the third corner of stewardship: making disciples.

Term to Remember: DISCIPLESHIP is the process of teaching Christians how to be obedient to Christ and all that the Bible teaches.

No one stated it better than Jesus Himself. After his resurrection, he met his disciples on a mountain in Galilee. He said, according to Matthew 28:19-20, *Therefore go and make disciples of all nations, baptizing them in the name of the Father and of the Son and of the Holy Spirit, and teaching them to obey everything I have commanded you. And surely I am with you always, to the very end of the age.*

This passage is often called The Great Commission, and we use it as the basis for our belief in evangelism. It is why most churches have at least some semblance of an outreach program. I say that because sadly, most of us aren't passionate enough about evangelism to leave our comfort zone and cross into the flames, as we talked about in Chapter Eleven. And Jesus here is adamant about us "going," but how many people really stop and ponder what else he said in those two short verses?

He didn't say "go and evangelize," although evangelism is obviously implied. He said "go and make disciples." Herein lies the reason for so much fog surrounding the church today. We love to see lost people come down the aisle of the church to give themselves to Christ. It's exciting! Sometimes it's someone for whom we've prayed over and over again. Maybe we have sent cards to that person, or visited him, or invited him to church. Maybe we witnessed to him and shared our testimony. Seeing someone realize, for the first time, his need for Christ and then boldly stepping forward is such a wonderful sight.

And we certainly love to see those new believers baptized. Baptism is one of the most touching and emotional moments in the life of a congregation. It even makes us cry sometimes. It is an act of obedience, wherein the new Christian publicly connects himself to the death, burial and resurrection of Jesus Christ. We make a big deal over baptism, as well we should. We, the church, make a big deal over a lost soul that is saved, and we make a big deal over their obedience in baptism. But do we make a big deal over their spiritual education?

Do we get just as excited about seeing that person show up for Sunday School as we did about seeing him in the baptismal waters? Do we make a big deal about making certain he has a good study Bible? Do we get excited about praying with our new brother in Christ? Do we bother to mentor him, or do we just send him into his spiritual journey and say, "Good luck!?" As I have mentioned before, God didn't put us on this earth and wish us luck. He intervened on our behalf all throughout human history. He does expect us to intervene on behalf of others. He expects us to make disciples.

The truth is, once that new believer comes up out of the baptismal waters, the easy part is done. The really hard part is just beginning, but the church seems to have forgotten the art of disciple-making. It is part of the forgotten truth about stewardship that we are responsible for the care and nurturing of those whom we reach with the gospel message of Jesus Christ.

Consider what Jesus said, again from Matthew 28:19, *baptizing them in the name of the Father and of the Son and of the Holy Spirit.* I believe Jesus was commanding us to baptize new Christians into a life of holiness. You must go back to what we covered in Chapter Five—Where Salvation Leads, concerning the tabernacle (later the temple). It was divided into three parts. The innermost part was the Holy of Holies. That corresponds to your soul, and at the point of salvation, God's Spirit comes to take up residence there. *Your body is a temple,* 1 Corinthians 6:19. The other part, just outside the Holy of Holies, was the Holy Place. It corresponds to your mind, or what the Hebrews called your spirit. We often call it your "heart." When you commit to letting God renew your mind, this is where the real work of discipleship happens—in your mind. This is where your thought patterns change and you learn to think of God as your Father, not your enemy. The outer part of the temple was the court, the place where blood sacrifices were offered.

Just as the temple bore a resemblance to God's Trinitarian nature, so do we. We have a soul, a mind, and a body. All three should be affected by our salvation, not just our soul. God's Spirit, indwelling your soul, is counseling you, convicting you, and confirming God's words to you. That should spill over into your mind, leading you to pursue holiness and transformation through the renewing of the mind. That, in turn, should spill over into your body, where your behavior and your actions begin to reflect what's happening deeper inside.

Think of it this way. Imagine the Holy Spirit in your soul singing Reginald Heber's great majestic hymn, "Holy, Holy, Holy." As a Christian, this is in fact the mantra being sounded in your soul, proclaiming the presence of God in you, the temple. Imagine, however, that your mind has not been through the renewal process, and it is singing its own tune, Hank Williams' "I'm So Lonesome I Could Cry." It's a good song, a classic, but should not be the theme song of your mind in Christ. It would clash with what the Holy Spirit is singing in your soul.

Now imagine that while your soul is being serenaded by God's Spirit, and at the same time your mind is singing the blues, yet another theme is blaring from the actions of your body: Frank Sinatra's "I Did It My Way." Do you begin to understand the confusion inherent in that situation? In musical terms, it is called a cacophony, defined as disagreeable or discordant sounds. In other words, it's very unpleasant. A Christian living with three discordant theme songs is not a Christian at peace. In fact, to those on the outside looking in at your life, you are a picture of chaos.

Now, consider something Jesus did, according to Matthew 21:12-13. It is often misunderstood. *Jesus entered the temple area and drove out all who were buying and selling there. He overturned the tables of the money changers and the benches of those selling doves. "It is written," he said to them, "'My house will be called a house of prayer,' but you are making it a 'den of robbers.'"* Many Jews who lived outside Israel would travel to Jerusalem for the various religious festivals, and their foreign currency had to be exchanged for local currency. They also could purchase animals for sacrifice. These things alone were probably not sinful, but the location was. They had turned Solomon's outer court, the court of the Gentiles, into a marketplace.

You remember King Solomon's prayer of dedication after the temple was built, from Chapter Two? The outer court was intended to be a place where evangelism takes place, where Gentiles would come seeking the One True God. They would look towards the temple and pray, and Solomon asked God to answer their prayers so they would go home and tell others about the God who answers prayer. But now, this court had been turned into a marketplace. The Jewish worshipers seemed uninterested in evangelizing the nations. If a non-Jew were to approach this chaos, would he be convicted to pray? Would he find this appealing? Not likely. God had called this nation of people to lead others to the truth. They were robbing God of converts. This made Jesus angry and he rightfully ran them out. What was happening outside—what the lost world saw—did not match the holiness coming from inside the temple. Instead of a holy temple, the world saw a marketplace.

So it is in our own lives, when your behavior and actions do not reflect the holiness we claim to have in our souls, the very presence of God's Spirit. Your body is a temple, but is it functioning as a temple? Does your body appear to the outsider to be a "house of prayer," or does it look more like a shopping center? A tavern, perhaps or maybe a nightclub? A place of business or a place of worship? Tough questions, I know, but Jesus knows the truth about you, and what kind of image you project to the lost world. If it is not an image of worship, then your body is a *"den of robbers."* You were created in God's image and called to a high and noble purpose: to be a temple.

We are made to resemble our Father in His Trinitarian nature, by allowing his song in our souls to spill over into our minds and be translated out through our bodies. Then we transmit a message of peace and unity. That is what others should see in us, the harmonious life lived in Christ, not a cacophony. This is why Jesus told us to *make disciples,* and reminded us that our job is *teaching them to obey everything I have commanded you.* He wants us to teach holiness and transformation.

This is why so many Christians are not full of the joy they expected to come when they accepted Christ as their Savior. The soul is changed forever by the presence of God's Spirit, but the mind, for so many, is still singing a sad song. And though they may try very hard to behave like a Christian, there simply is not the support coming from the mind to make it feasible. Holiness must start in the soul and work its way through the mind and into the body. Many of us, myself included, grew up hearing sermons telling us to "straighten up and act right," as one evangelist liked to say. But that teaching implied that behavior of the body would lead to holiness, as if acting holy on the outside would make us holy on the inside.

That's like saying to the Jew that if they made sacrifices in the court, **then** the priests would feel compelled to go in the Holy Place to offer prayers, and **then** God would come into the Holy of Holies and **then** the whole temple would become holy. That's backwards! The Spirit of God was **already** in the Holy of Holies! Otherwise, the sacrifices made would have been meaningless and empty. The entire temple area had **already** been declared a holy place by God himself. And God demanded holiness there. Likewise, if you are saved, God's spirit is **already** in your soul and your mind and your body have **already** been declared a holy place. If you are not pursuing that holiness, you are being disobedient.

You may be reading this and realizing that it describes your life. You are not alone. I have been there. In fact, I spent a couple of decades as a discordant Christian. The theme song in my soul was not the same one playing in my mind or my body. Unfortunately, I was surrounded by Christians suffering the same way, so they didn't recognize anything unusual about me. No one confronted me about it, because in spite of the cacophony, I was living a relatively clean life. But make no mistake—I was not holy! And I knew it. And yes, it affected other people. I was robbing God.

You may be reading this and thinking, "It doesn't matter what I do or how I think, or how I live my life. I'm not hurting anybody!" That's absolutely wrong. If you are a discordant Christian, with holiness in your soul and unholiness driving your thoughts and actions, what kind of witness are you to the lost? You are hurting the cause of Christ by implying with your life that chaos is normal—that holiness and transformation are optional—that doing everything Jesus taught isn't really necessary. You may be like that pastor I mentioned who said to me, "I know what the Bible says, but that's not how we're going to do it." If so, you may be doing more harm for the church than good.

The lost man does not have a holy theme song playing in his mind, because God's Spirit doesn't dwell there. He is lost, and without Christ is headed for eternal hell, but on this earth at least he is consistent. What plays in his soul matches what is in his mind and his actions. Don't be mistaken here. Being a "good person" is not the same as holiness. God says that without salvation *even our righteous acts are like filthy rags*, Isaiah 64:6. The redeemed man, on the other hand, is commanded to have a holy theme song in his soul, mind and body. He then takes on the resemblance of his heavenly Father's Trinitarian nature, and projects unity and harmony, a witness to the dramatic changing power of the gospel. Thus his life here on earth is also consistent.

So the lost man is consistent, and the saved man, pursuing holiness, is consistent. The lost man is consistently pointing people away from God, while the saved man, pursuing holiness, is pointing people toward God. It is the discordant Christian, the in-betweener, who does the most harm to the church, because he claims to be saved by the glorious power of the gospel, yet lives a defeated life. This is why Jesus said to the church at Laodicea, in Revelation 3:15-16, *I know your deeds, that you are neither cold nor hot. I wish you were either one or the other! So, because you are lukewarm—neither hot nor cold—I am about to spit you out of my mouth.* God doesn't like it when we accept His great gift of salvation in order to escape hell and then refuse his call to holiness and transformation. He doesn't like that at all, because it hinders the gospel message. Lost people are not drawn to a message of hope that apparently doesn't deliver, and that's the mixed message we send when we claim salvation but reject holiness.

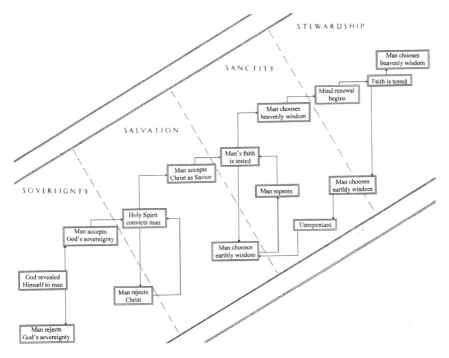

STEWARDSHIP

At some point, the discordant Christian will grow weary of the constant internal conflict and seek some kind of resolution. He may feel convicted about it, but without a mentor, a disciple-maker, to offer discernment, he may conclude that his salvation experience wasn't genuine. He may walk down the aisle again, be baptized again, but soon he finds himself dealing with the same old internal conflict.

We pastors often preach that if your behavior isn't holy you are not really saved. Sometimes that is the case, but often it is not. We must be aware of how the holiness process takes place in the Christian. The church has often wrongly assumed, as I mentioned before, that at the point of salvation auto-pilot takes over and holiness just happens. It doesn't. Even when you are saved, holiness is a choice. Renewal of the mind is a process you must be engaged in.

In many cases, the discordant Christian will get tired and frustrated with the lack of progress or change in his life and simply give up. Then he becomes what we call back-slidden. He may or may not attend church anymore. Either way, he is checked out emotionally. If he continues to attend church, he does so strictly out of a sense of obligation.

Now, try to imagine a congregation full of discordant Christians, not all of them, mind you, but many of them. Perhaps a majority even. They want to be right with God, but haven't been taught how. They are Christians, but they are not **disciples**! As such, they do not know the difference between earthly thinking and heavenly thinking. They do not know how to rely on the power, wisdom and understanding of God. Consequently, they are probably not very effective, if at all, at evangelism. After all, who would be excited about sharing the transformational message of the gospel, if they don't feel transformed by it themselves? You have just imagined the fog I was describing in Part One, the fog in which I grew up, and the fog in which I have served in previous churches.

Now imagine what these discordant Christians are going to bring to your church's next business meeting. They will bring conflict. They will bring earthly thinking. They will bring their dependence on human power, and all its human limitations. They will bring their dependence on human wisdom and human understanding. They will not urge the church to prayer, because they have been asking God to fix them for years and feel that their prayers were futile. They will not say with confidence, as Jehoshaphat did, *"We do not know what to do, but our eyes are upon you."* They may not mean any harm, but their minds have not been transformed. They have not been properly taught to obey, as Jesus said, *everything I have commanded you.* They are like sheep wandering in the pasture without a shepherd.

2 Peter 2:20-22 addresses this problem in the church. Peter wrote, *If they have escaped the corruption of the world by knowing our Lord and Savior Jesus Christ and are again entangled in it and overcome, they are worse off at the end than they were at the beginning. It would have been better for them not to have known the way of righteousness, than to have known it and then turn their backs on the sacred command that was passed on to them. Of them the parables are true: "A dog returns to its vomit," and "A sow that is washed goes back to her wallowing in the mud."* Whether intentional or not, these

discordant Christians do much damage to the church and the cause of Christ.

When we do not make disciples and that corner of stewardship sags or collapses, it has a domino affect on the other corners. The next corner to fall is usually discipline. Discordant Christians don't practice discipline, at least not well. Earthly wisdom becomes very enticing. "If it works for corporate America why can't it work for the church?" they may ask. The last corner to fall is usually evangelism. The conflict and confusion, saddled with the lack of heavenly empowerment, make our evangelistic efforts ineffective. Eventually, we may even give up on evangelism, relegating our outreach ministry to postings on the church sign. That's why we are not winning America to Christ. Signs don't win people to Christ—walking temples do!

There is one more corner of stewardship—Priorities. I placed it last because when the other three corners are safe and secure our priorities naturally fall into place. Transformed, holy Christians will naturally align their priorities. Consequently, however, priorities are usually the first corner to show cracks when the church begins to drift spiritually. Our priorities are the first warning sign of weakness in the church.

CHAPTER TWELVE

STEWARDSHIP IS PRIORITIES

We have established the difference between transformed Christians, or disciples, and discordant Christians. There is no implication here that a disciple is perfect—far from it! But he is pursuing holiness, not simply by trying to "act right" but by allowing Biblical truths to change him, to renew his mind. In Chapter Five we learned about transformation, and made use of the passage from Romans 12:1, *Therefore, I urge you, brothers, in view of God's mercy, to offer your bodies as living sacrifices, holy and pleasing to God—this is your spiritual act of worship.* The disciple is not perfect, but he is determined to be a living sacrifice.

That's why I teach that we can try to clean up our behavior first, but without a change in mindset, the good behavior isn't likely to last. God's word in Romans 12 is teaching us that our priorities will fall naturally in line with God's desires once our minds are in sync with God and our bodies are following. In other words, our time, talent and money will be our living sacrifices.

This is why our sermons on stewardship rarely effect any real or permanent change in behavior. We are asking Christians, many of whom are discordant, to give their time, talent and money to God's ongoing mission work in the church. They typical listener, if he is not transformed, may hear the message and recognize the truth in it, and it does appeal to his soul's theme song of holiness, because God's Spirit is present there. The message clashes, however, with the music playing in his mind. If his mind still reverts back regularly to that old way of thinking, as if God is his enemy, then why would he feel compelled to give more of himself to God's work?

Recall Colossians 1:21, which we looked at in Chapter Seven. It says, *once you were alienated from God and were enemies in your minds because of your evil behavior.* Keep in mind what we learned about the four ways in which Scripture tells us we think of God before our minds are renewed. Romans 8:5-8 teach that our minds are *set on what nature desires,* and on *death.* It also teaches that *the sinful mind is hostile to God,* and *cannot please God.* The discordant Christian is not yet living in accordance with the Spirit. So, when the pastor urges him to be a good steward, his private answer may be something like this: "I've given a lot to God and he isn't making things work out for me!" or something of that nature.

The Christian who is not undergoing the transformation process is rarely content with his circumstances. More often than not, he is frustrated by what he views as a lack of intervention on God's part. When conflict surfaces in his home, his family, his job, or his finances, it may never occur to him that the conflict in his life is connected to the internal conflict between his soul, mind and body. He will not likely recognize that the lack of peace probably stems from his lack of holiness and his lack of spiritual growth. No, the discordant Christian will blame other people or God for his circumstances. Proverbs 19:23 says it so well. *The fear of the Lord leads to life: Then one rests content, untouched by trouble.* We saw the word fear earlier, when we talked about discipline. Psalm 111:10 says *The fear of the Lord is the beginning of wisdom.* It does not mean we must be afraid of God as Christians, scared of being destroyed at a moment's notice. It means to hold him in reverence and awe, to recognize his sovereignty, his power, wisdom and understanding. That is the key to contentment, because when you rely on him, the burden no longer rests on your shoulders.

But the Christian who is out of sync is rarely content. He may look around at the congregation on Sunday morning, noticing the businessman or woman, doctor or wealthy older couple, and think to himself, "They can afford to pay for all this stuff. Let them do it. God has given them more than their share." When politicians try to invoke that type of envy we call it class warfare, but Satan invented this tactic, and he uses it in the church to great effect.

The discordant Christian will hear the pastor say that he must put God first in his life, but he will look around at all the things absorbing his time and think, "If God would bless me I wouldn't have to work so hard. Then I would have time to come up here to the church and do stuff." He doesn't even realize that the church isn't a place—it's a people. He is the church. He is one member of a greater body and when any member refuses to serve his purpose, the body suffers. The body becomes functionally disabled.

This type of Christian constitutes a large percentage of the church today. Some well-known evangelists have asserted that most of our congregants are actually lost. They suggest fifty to eighty percent are not really saved. That may be true, but I don't think that is always the case. I believe many, like me, walked down the aisle because they knew God was speaking to them. I believe many made a sincere prayer and confession before God, asking Jesus Christ to be their personal Savior. I also believe most of them, like me, were not taught much beyond that. This book is not written to the lost world, though it is my prayer that some will come to Christ because of it. Rather, though, this book comes from a deep conviction that the church has forgotten some basic and important truths, and is not functioning properly as a result.

The discordant Christian does not recognize the utter and total sovereignty of God Almighty. He does not know that salvation is not the end of his spiritual quest, but only the beginning. He does not know that he is called to sanctity—that God wants to change not only his future eternal status, but his current status as well. He does not know that holiness through Christ Jesus working in your mind and body is the key to having peace, joy and contentment. Without these basic truths, he will not know if his shepherd is teaching him truth or folly. He will lack discernment. He certainly will not know the profound wisdom of stewardship. He can know all these things, however, once he becomes a disciple.

I shared in the previous chapter my belief that when one corner sags it exerts undue pressure on the others. The four corners of stewardship all work together to support the ministry of the church. The church must be in the business of winning people to Christ. A passion for evangelism builds a strong corner to support ministry. The church must also discipline itself to be totally dependent on God. Calling on his power, wisdom and understanding leads to heavenly thinking and sheds earthly thinking.

Thus a second strong corner is established. The church that is winning people to Christ and trusting in God will want to make new converts into disciples. It will teach them holiness and transformation. This type of church will have its priorities in line, because a church that practices good stewardship of evangelism, discipline and discipleship will naturally practice good stewardship of its time, talent and money. Disciples are more interested in the things of God than the things of man. They won't serve out of guilt but out of joy. They won't donate because of some sense of obligation, but will be cheerful givers. Discordant Christians look for ways to avoid service. They often live life wondering how much God will allow them to get away with before He starts chastising. Disciples want to please God because they feel loved by Him.

PART FOUR REVIEW

Terms to Remember:

STEWARDSHIP—taking care of something that is valuable

EVANGELISM—spreading the gospel of Jesus Christ

DISCIPLINE—choosing to seek God's heavenly wisdom and reject earthly wisdom

DISCIPLESHIP—teaching new Christians how to live for Christ

PART FIVE

THE
TRUTH
ABOUT
SHEPHERDS

CHAPTER THIRTEEN

HOW TO SPOT A HIRELING

One of the first sermons I ever preached was titled "The True Shepherd." I wasn't a pastor then, but still Minister of Music, Education, and Outreach. As I shared with you in the introduction, our pastor had left to take another position, and so we were without a pastor or even an interim for six months. Our search committee had found a man who they decided was God's choice to be our next pastor, and he had spent the previous weekend getting to know our church. He preached a couple of sermons, ate dinner with the staff and the deacons, answered questions and so forth. Then our church took a week to pray about it, and on this Sunday we were voting.... and I was preaching.

Another man in our church, himself a former pastor, had been asked to preach this day, but could not due to health issues, and so I was given the opportunity to deliver a sermon. God had not yet made it clear to me that I was called to be a pastor, but it was clear to me that I enjoyed teaching and preaching, so I looked forward to this Sunday. I had been leading a men's bible study, teaching through the gospel of Mark, so I had plenty of study material to glean from, and chose a sermon topic that I thought appropriate for the occasion. However, God woke me early that Sunday morning and changed my sermon entirely.

I had planned to preach about Jesus the Healer, from Mark 2, but instead God turned my attention to Jesus the Provider, from Mark 6, where Jesus fed the 5,000 men. That was only half of the message, however, the first half coming from Ezekiel 34.

In this chapter of Ezekiel, verses 1-6, God sends a very pointed and harsh message to the spiritual leaders, or shepherds, of Israel. *The word of the Lord came to me: "Son of man, prophesy against the shepherds of Israel; prophesy and say to them: This is what the Sovereign Lord says: Woe to the shepherds of Israel who only take care of themselves! Should not shepherds take care of the flock? You eat the curds, clothe yourselves with the wool and slaughter the choice animals, but you do not take care of the flock. You have not strengthened the weak or healed the sick or bound up the injured. You have not brought back the strays or searched for the lost. You have ruled them harshly and brutally. So they were scattered because there was no shepherd, and when they were scattered they became food for all the wild animals. My sheep wandered over all the mountains and on every high hill. They were scattered over the whole earth, and no one searched or looked for them."*

God was speaking directly to the spiritual leaders of the old covenant, but it still applies to the spiritual leaders of the new covenant. It applies to the church. Read what Jesus said in John 10:11-13: *I am the good shepherd. The good shepherd lays down his life for the sheep. The hired hand* (hireling in the KJV) *is not the shepherd who owns the sheep. So when he sees the wolf coming, he abandons the sheep and runs away. Then the wolf attacks the flock and scatters it. The man runs away because he is a hired hand and cares nothing for the sheep.* Many pastors today like to call themselves shepherds, but do they heed God's words to the shepherds? Are they willing to live up to the standard set by Christ himself? Are they willing to yield to God's sovereignty, teach salvation, and dedicate themselves to modeling sanctity? Do they read the words of Ezekiel 34 and ask themselves, "Am I really taking care of the flock?" Do they read the words of Jesus in John 10 and ask themselves, "Am I a hireling or a shepherd?"

This passage explains the source of the fog I talked about in Part One—being in the church but not knowing our purpose—lacking vision or direction, watching people fall away from their faith and wander away from the church. God says it is because we lack true shepherds that we become vulnerable, *food for all the wild animals*. What did He mean by that? 1 Peter 5:8 says, *Your enemy the devil prowls around like a roaring lion looking for someone to devour.* Poor leadership leaves our churches weak and defenseless. God was telling me, through this sermon, that we are missing the truth about our leadership, and this lack of truth is taking the life out of our congregations. It is making us vulnerable to Satan's attacks. He is literally picking us off, one by one. The church seems to have forgotten the **truth about shepherds.**

Term to Remember: a SHEPHERD is one appointed by God to care for his people. It applies to anyone in leadership, but especially to ministers.

So, what does a false shepherd look like? How does he behave? Let's examine the list from Ezekiel 34. According to verse 2, a false shepherd only takes care of himself. It's not that he doesn't show up and preach, or visit a church member in the hospital. In fact, he might be a really nice guy, but his heart isn't truly in it. He puts himself above the flock, or congregation. I once served under a pastor who admitted openly that his first desire was for a completely different career, but when that didn't work out, he decided to try ministry. I don't believe he was truly called to the ministry. He was a nice guy, I respected the fact that he was my leader, and I loved him, but our church was probably the foggiest one I've ever been part of. We were not growing in our knowledge of the Lord. We were shrinking numerically. People were falling away. We lacked vision or direction, and the congregation knew it. Most of them didn't really know why, but they were constantly asking "what's wrong here?" When church members sense that there is a problem, and start asking questions, the false shepherd will certainly find someone to blame, anyone but himself. Then the feeding frenzy begins. It was sad to watch.

Shepherds are often the problem in the church, but seldom aware of it. If they recognize that their church has a problem they often assume it is the flock. A minister I once knew had the habit of saying, "ministry would be fun if it weren't for the people!" Ministry is all about people. You serve the Lord, your Master, by serving his church, and his church **is** people. If your heart isn't in it, if you are not truly called by God to minister, then you will probably put yourself above the flock, and when problems arise, you will blame them, but never yourself. In verse 3, God explains that the false shepherd lives well off of the flock, using them to meet his physical and financial needs, but giving little, or nothing, in return. I am told that the average tenure for a pastor in Southern Baptist churches is 2 or 3 years, and similar in other denominations. It seems most pastors are always serving one church while looking for the next one. And, not surprisingly, the next church is almost always bigger and pays more. It is rare indeed for a shepherd to leave one flock for a smaller one. It seems, in our modern church anyway, that God never calls anyone to make sacrifices, especially financial sacrifices. That's a pattern you won't find in the New Testament, by the way. Should churches take care of their leaders? Absolutely! But every leader should always put God's desires above his own.

In verse 4, God says that the false shepherd does not strengthen the weak. Every church has weak members, usually because they have not been well-taught or loved. A false shepherd will feel contempt for these people rather than compassion. He may be polite in public, but take him aside and you will quickly find out how he really feels. Every pastor needs someone he can confide in and share his frustrations with, but a false shepherd will usually not be able to keep his frustrations limited to a small circle of confidants. Verse 4 also tells us that the false shepherd will not heal the sick or bind the injured. I don't think God necessarily is talking about miraculous healing of disease, although I do not discount the possibility. I think he is talking about those church members who have spiritual problems that require much prayer and teaching, and those who have perhaps been hurt by bad experiences in church. Every congregation has members with "injured" hearts. They've been hurt, disappointed, let down. A false shepherd makes little or no effort to address these injuries, usually because it demands too much time or effort. It's just as well to him if these people go find another church.

Verse 4 also tells us that a false shepherd does not make much effort to bring back church members who have fallen away, or to go after the lost in the community. As a staff member, I led the outreach ministry at two different churches, under three different pastors, and only one of those pastors actually participated in our church outreach program. One of them told me outright, "that's just not my gig." Another one said, "that's your job, not mine." I'm not implying that they never made a visit or call, and they did encourage the congregation, from the pulpit, to get involved in outreach, but they didn't actually show up themselves. And guess what? When the pastor isn't passionate about it, the congregation won't be either.

In fact, this is one of the big truths I learned in my years of "second-tier" leadership. No matter how hard I worked at leading a music ministry, education, or outreach ministry, my results always were limited by my pastor. The congregation will not go any deeper spiritually than their pastor. A few will, of course, but as a whole, they will go only as far, or as high, as the pastor leads them. I call it the Stained-Glass Ceiling. Believe me, I spent a few years beating my head on that ceiling, and it doesn't break. The pastor, or senior pastor, truly does set the tone for the whole church. If his heart isn't in it, the church will wander *over all the mountains*.

The last thing God said in verse 4 is that the false shepherd rules the church harshly and brutally. The truth is, ministry is hard. Maintaining your patience with the spiritually weak, or biblically ignorant, is hard. Strengthening their knowledge and growing their faith is hard. Showing compassion to those who are spiritually sick is hard. Taking care of the spiritually injured, binding their wounds and nursing them back to health is hard. Building relationships with those who have wandered from the church is hard. Reaching the lost in the surrounding community is hard. Harsh attitudes and brutal leadership simply will not get the job done. I have seen churches grow under such leadership, because some people are drawn to a dictatorial pastorate, but I have yet to see that growth maintained. At some point it falls apart, usually when the overbearing pastor leaves.

A false shepherd simply isn't willing to exert much effort on the flock. He would prefer that those he deems "high-maintenance" go find another church. Anyone who doesn't agree with his agenda can go find another church. Anyone with a complaint can go find another church. If the church is in an urban area, or a town where new residents are moving in regularly, he can probably get away with that attitude, because there will always be new people showing up to replace the ones who leave. That is not a biblical attitude, but I have witnessed it all my life. It is not the pastor's job to decide who he will and will not minister to. If there are people in the church who are causing problems and genuinely need to leave, I have found that prayer is the best solution.

As a music minister, I once encountered just such a person. He was a nice fellow who started attending our church, but he seemed to carry a chip on his shoulder. He appeared to have a critical nature about him, but I, and others in the church, accepted him and loved him anyway. However, he started bringing his tambourine to the worship services. Now, I like exciting worship, and we were slightly contemporary anyway, sometimes using a tambourine here and there, so the instrument wasn't the problem. The problem was that he was trying to lead, vicariously, from the pew. He was trying to take our worship in a direction that neither I the worship leader, nor our pastor, felt led to go. So I prayed that day, during the invitation, a simple prayer: "Dear Father, if I am wrong, show me I am wrong, and thank you for bringing this man into our fellowship. However, if he is wrong, show him he is wrong, or have him find another church where he is needed. In Jesus' name I pray, amen." After that service, I never saw that guy again.

That happened at the first church I served, where I was so blessed to have a pastor who really believed in prayer. He taught me to surrender those things to prayer. I believe God honors the prayer life of a church when the pastor is a praying man himself. A false shepherd will be a hindrance to the prayer life and spiritual growth of the church he is supposedly leading.

I believe that most pastors are genuine. I personally know quite a few who are remarkable men of faith,with great compassion, and love for the gospel. They work hard, study hard, and pray hard. I believe that hirelings are the exception to the rule, but they do exist. The true shepherds are human, however, and we are all susceptible to thinking the wrong way, especially when we become discouraged. This is why the renewing of the mind is so critical, especially for shepherds. Our job in God's plan is to lead people down the path of understanding. We have to teach the sovereignty of God, the salvation of God, the sanctity of God, and the stewardship of God's church. It requires wisdom and understanding. Pray for your pastor. God has given him a great and mighty task!

This passage from Ezekiel 34 is harsh. But God is only harsh because his plan of redemption is so important; and remember, God protects what he loves. He protects his plan and protects his people. In verse 10 God says this: *I am against the shepherds and will hold them accountable for my flock.* Being a shepherd is serious business. In fact, it is God's business. So God has harsh words for any of us who serve in that capacity but fail to take it seriously. That's why your pastor needs your prayers. God holds him accountable for his service to the church.

JESUS THE GOOD SHEPHERD

Jesus encountered the false shepherds of Israel over and over in his ministry. The Pharisees were a religious group with great intentions but poor results, and the teachers of the law, or scribes, were charged with interpreting, teaching, and maintaining the scripture. Both groups were scolded harshly by Jesus, and both groups tried desperately to undermine his ministry, even to the desire to kill him. Did you catch that? Jesus' greatest opposition didn't come from Gentiles, but from his fellow Jews. Not from the pagan Roman government but his fellow religious leaders. False shepherds do lots of damage because they work within the church rather than attack it from the outside.

Matthew 23 records Jesus' words concerning these false shepherds. *Then Jesus said to the crowds and to his disciples: "The teachers of the law and the Pharisees sit in Moses' seat. So you must obey them and do everything they tell you. But do not do what they do, for they do not practice what they preach. They tie up heavy loads and put them on men's shoulders, but they themselves are not willing to lift a finger to move them."* Furthermore, Jesus referred to them as *hypocrites*, verse 13, *blind guides*, verse 16, *snakes and vipers*, verse 33. His words are harsh, but reflect the tone of Ezekiel 34, verse10, where God said, *I am against the shepherds and will hold them accountable for my flock.* Jesus fulfilled that prophecy literally when he confronted the Pharisees and the teachers of the law for being false shepherds. It is harsh because the results of their falsehood were harsh. Jesus was holding them accountable. In Luke 11:52, Jesus said, *Woe to you experts in the law, because you have taken away the key to knowledge. You yourselves have not entered, and you have hindered those who were entering.* Do you realize what Jesus was saying? Do you realize the result of poor shepherding? God had given ample prophecy in the Old Testament for the Jewish people to recognize their Messiah when he appeared, but the Jewish shepherds had not done their job of teaching the scripture and leading the people. Most of the

Jewish people did not recognize Jesus as the Messiah and for those who did, the Pharisees and the teachers of the law became a stumbling block. Rather than clearly seeing Jesus as the fulfillment of scripture, most of them were overcome by the fog.

So, you may be wondering by now, what does Ezekiel 34 have to do with Mark 6, and Jesus feeding the five thousand? Jesus was the perfect example of a true shepherd. He took care of physical weakness, physical sickness, and physical injury to prove He was God, but he also provided spiritual truth to take care of spiritual weakness, sickness, and injury. He did both.

Ezekiel 34:11-12 says, *For this is what the Sovereign Lord says: "I myself will search for my sheep and look after them. As a shepherd looks after his scattered flock when he is with them, so will I look after my sheep."*

God promised something very significant here. He promised to shepherd his people personally. There is a coming dispensation, the Kingdom Age, where Jesus will reign over the earth after his second coming, and I believe God is alluding to that time. But I believe he was also pointing to something Israel would see much sooner: Jesus' first coming. That's where Mark 6 comes in. Verses 39-44 record this miracle. *Then Jesus directed them to have all the people sit down in groups on the green grass. So they sat down in groups of hundreds and fifties. Taking the five loaves and the two fish and looking up to heaven, he gave thanks and broke the loaves. Then he gave them to his disciples to set before the people. He also divided the two fish among them all. They all ate and were satisfied, and the disciples picked up twelve basketfuls of broken pieces of bread and fish. The number of the men who had eaten was five thousand.*

Jesus fulfilled the prophecy of Ezekiel literally. *I will tend them in a good pasture, and the mountain heights of Israel will be their grazing land. There they will lie down in good grazing land, and there they will feed in a rich pasture on the mountains of Israel* Ezekiel 34:14. Jesus literally fed the sheep (the people) on the green grass.

This was the message of the sermon God gave me that Sunday that we were voting on a new pastor. God was teaching me, and our church, what a true shepherd should look like and how he should function, and what a false shepherd looks like and how he functions.

CHAPTER FOURTEEN

TRUE LEADERSHIP

There are certain hallmarks of true shepherds. I think Simon Peter is perhaps one of the best examples of true leadership. He wasn't perfect—not at all. Leaders never are, and we should never hold them in such high regard that we think them infallible. Likewise, we should never punish them unduly for their imperfections. In fact, let me be clear on this point: I consider myself blessed to have served in the music ministry under four different pastors. It was a blessing to observe their ministries up close and personal. As such, I saw the strengths and weaknesses of each, but do not mistake my observations for criticism, as I am all too aware of my own weaknesses as a pastor. However, God did use those times to teach me and mold me, and each pastor, in his own way, was part of that process. So I am not only grateful to them, but I genuinely love each of them. Many great men are disqualified because they make a mistake. It doesn't have to be that way. Let's examine Peter's track record.

Leaders make mistakes, but they learn from those mistakes. Peter was a leader among Jesus' disciples, and yet he was weak when Jesus was on trial. He denied even knowing Jesus, just as Jesus had said he would. Matthew 26:71-72 tells us, *Then he went out to the gateway, where another girl saw him and said to the people there, "This fellow was with Jesus of Nazareth." He denied it again, with an oath: "I don't know the man!"* Peter made a big mistake that night, but like I said, Jesus knew it would happen. In fact, Jesus said something very important to him earlier, recorded in Luke 22:31-32, *"Simon, Simon, Satan has asked to sift you as wheat. But I have prayed for you, Simon, that your faith may not fail. And when you have turned back, strengthen your brothers.*"

Jesus knew Peter would make that mistake, but prayed that Peter would learn from his mistake and use what he learned to teach others. Peter did just that. His first epistle, 1 Peter, opens with this greeting: *Peter, an apostle of Jesus Christ....* The man, who once claimed not to even know Jesus, is here boldly professing himself to be one of His apostles. Church history suggests that Peter was crucified, martyred because of his unwavering faith in Jesus. Jesus himself alluded to this, recorded in John 21:18-19. *"I tell you the truth, when you were younger you dressed yourself and went where you wanted; but when you are old you will stretch out your hands, and someone else will dress you and lead you where you do not want to go." Jesus said this to indicate the kind of death by which Peter would glorify God. Then he said to him, "Follow me!"*

Peter learned from his mistake. He went from denial to martyrdom, but in between, he did a few other things that true leaders do. Peter, like all true leaders, was an encourager. Consider his words to the church in 1 Peter 1:3-9. It is a beautiful passage chock full of encouraging truths. *Praise be to the God and Father of our Lord Jesus Christ! In his great mercy he has given us new birth into a living hope through the resurrection of Jesus Christ from the dead, and into an inheritance that can never perish, spoil or fade—kept in heaven for you, who through faith are shielded by God's power until the coming of the salvation that is ready to be revealed in the last time. In this you greatly rejoice, though now for a little while you may have had to suffer grief in all kinds of trials. These have come so that your faith—of greater worth than gold, which perishes even though refined by fire—may be proved genuine and may result in praise, glory and honor when Jesus Christ is revealed. Though you have not seen him, you love him; and even though you do not see him now, you believe in him and are filled with an inexpressible and glorious joy, for you are receiving the goal of your faith, the salvation of your souls.*

Peter is writing to the scattered church, primarily Jews who have accepted Christ as their Savior. The persecution and scattering of the church would have opened the door to great discouragement to these believers, but Peter's words are full of encouragement. Not just empty words, but rock-solid spiritual truths; serious words for serious times, but very encouraging. Peter is an encouraging leader.

Point: Leaders encourage us!

Peter also exhibits the leadership trait of being an educator. In 1 Peter 1:14-16, he is teaching fundamental doctrine. *As obedient children, do not conform to the evil desires you had when you lived in ignorance. But just as he who called you is holy, so be holy in all you do; for it is written: "Be holy, because I am holy."* Peter here is quoting Leviticus 11:44. He is reminding them of the law God gave them under the old covenant, its call to holiness, and that it still applies. He is teaching them the truth about sanctity. He continues on, teaching them that the new covenant is greater than the old. He teaches them that Christ's redeeming work was planned before creation. He is teaching them the truth about salvation, and about sovereignty. He expounds on these truths in the remainder of his letter.

Point: Leaders educate us!

There is another trait of true leaders, again exhibited in the writing of Peter. True leaders expect their followers to change. A really good leader is never happy with the status quo. If he is willing to encourage you, and educate you, then he expects you to become a better person as a result. He said to the church, again in 1 Peter 1:22, *Now that you have purified yourselves by obeying the truth so that you have sincere love for your brothers, love one another deeply, from the heart.* He expects them to be obedient to the truth he is teaching them, and expects them to change, to grow in their love. He goes on to tell them to *rid yourselves of all malice and all deceit, hypocrisy, envy, and slander of every kind. Like newborn babies, crave pure spiritual milk, so that by it you may grow up in your salvation, now that you have tasted that the Lord is good.* 1 Peter 2:1-2.

Peter does not expect them to be content with what they know about God, or content with their level of commitment, or content with the depth of their love. He expects them to change, to grow, to learn more, to love more, to be stronger and more faithful Christians. True leaders are like that. Sometimes, church members don't want to change or grow. They may not think they need to, but a true leader will always challenge you to change.

Point: Leaders expect us to become better!

True shepherds are leaders. They learn from their mistakes. They encourage us, they educate us, and they expect us to respond to their leadership. I believe that true shepherds are also prophets, though not in the sense that most people think of prophecy. Prophecy, as in Old Testament prophecy, often involved seeing into the future, telling God's people what God intended to do. Many times, however, this prophecy was merely reminding God's people of things he had already told them. Many Old Testament prophecies concerned judgments on Israel if they failed to live up to God's commands, but these judgments had been clearly spelled out earlier in the scripture. The Jewish people always knew, as we mentioned in Part One, that disobedience would lead to punishment. Some prophecies, especially those concerning Jesus and his first coming, as well as his second coming, are truly future-telling. Since the bible is a complete work, giving us all we need to know about God and his plan of redemption, I do not believe the gift of prophecy still exists, at least not in the sense of more written revelation.

Term to Remember: PROPHECY is the gift of transmitting information from God to God's people, whether it is information about the past, present, or even the future.

I do, however, believe the gift of prophesy still exists, in the sense of reminding God's people of things he has already told us. I do believe that God speaks to prophets, or shepherds, and gives them messages for his church. In Revelation 1:20, Jesus explained a vision that John saw and was told to record. Jesus said, *The seven stars are the angels of the seven churches…* The Greek word rendered "angels" literally means "messengers" but has the implication here of "pastors." In the very next verse, Chapter 2:1, Jesus said, *"To the angel of the church in Ephesus, write:"*

Some want to believe that the word "angel" in these verses implies a heavenly angel assigned to guard over each church. It seems improbable, though, that Jesus would tell John to write down a message to send to a heavenly angel. Angels are themselves messengers of God, and do not require human mediators to be given their orders. These were actual letters, addressed to actual churches that really did exist at that time, and so it is far more logical to assume that Jesus was referring to the leaders of the churches, the shepherds. In each letter, Jesus tells the pastor, or shepherd, of each church what their church is doing right and/or wrong. In other words, God does use the local pastor to deliver his message to the local congregation. This is the gift of prophecy that I believe every true shepherd should possess. When the church comes together to worship, they should hear a message from God, relevant to their circumstances, delivered by their shepherd, one of God's messengers. This is one reason why your pastor needs your prayers. He carries a great responsibility to communicate God's heart to God's church.

Question: How often do you pray for your pastor? He has a great responsibility to God and to God's people. It is not an easy task.

PASTORS AS PROPHETS

There are some commonalities between the prophets who wrote parts of the bible and the prophets (pastors) who teach the Bible today. Prophets are not like other Christians, for the simple fact that they have a hard time ignoring God. Most Christians hear from God through the preaching of the scripture, through their own study of the scripture, and through their prayer time. They also have the indwelling Holy Spirit to counsel and convict. They can, if they wish, choose to neglect or ignore all of these! In fact, many Christians do just that. That is why we have discussed in this book holiness and transformation, because these are vital if we are to communicate with God. Unfortunately, it is quite easy to get lazy and fall away from these practices. It is not as easy for prophets, because God seems to speak to them more directly, more in-the-face, if you will.

You may find it quite easy to lose interest in church, and may get frustrated because your pastor urges you to be passionate. He is not doing that to irritate you. He is doing that because **he** is passionate about the church and wants you to share that passion. If he is truly called by God to be a pastor, then he is passionate because God won't let him be anything but passionate. Losing interest in church is not an option for him.

Jeremiah was a great prophet, but sometimes called a reluctant prophet. Being a prophet means telling people things they don't always want to hear. It can be frightening. Jeremiah said to God, *"Ah, Sovereign Lord," I said, "I do not know how to speak; I am only a child."* Jeremiah 1:6. God did not accept his objection. Verses 7 and 8 record God's response. *But the Lord said to me, "Do not say, 'I am only a child.' You must go to everyone I send you to and say whatever I command you. Do not be afraid of them, for I am with you and will rescue you," declares the Lord.*

At this point, Jeremiah had not said that he was afraid of the people, but God knew he would be. Church people can be intimidating. They can make a pastor's life difficult and put undue pressure on his family. They can threaten to get him fired, tarnish his reputation and leave him stigmatized. King Saul, the first king of Israel, disobeyed God out of fear of people. 1 Samuel 15:24 explains it: *Then Saul said to Samuel, "I have sinned. I violated the Lord's command and your instructions. I was afraid of the people and so I gave in to them."* When you find yourself criticizing your pastor, remember the pressure he is under. Saul was a king with almost unlimited authority and yet he buckled under the pressure of leading God's people. Imagine the stress your pastor feels trying to lead the typical church with the limited amount of authority he is allowed. It is not an easy task.

I have heard pastors talk about certain issues or sermon topics that they considered off-limits. "I would lose my job if I preached that!" Most people are uncomfortable with public speaking. Now imagine getting up in front of 50 people, or 500 people, or 5,000 people, every Sunday to tell them things that may be difficult to hear. If you are a true shepherd, a prophet or messenger, and God tells you to preach something, you HAVE to preach it, regardless of the repercussions. I have preached sermons at my church that I did not want to preach. I thought the messages were too harsh, but I never felt the freedom to skip these sermons. In fact, the sermons that scare me are often the ones that have the most impact. After a message like that, someone always comes to me afterward and says something like this: "That message was for me. I needed to hear the truth." In that case, we are both blessed. But don't miss this point: sometimes your pastor has to preach things he doesn't really want to. He needs your prayers to have courage.

A prophet, such as Jeremiah, receives messages directly from God, often with detailed instructions, and this is difficult to ignore. Have you heard of Jonah? He was a prophet who ignored God's instructions. Maybe you've heard what God did to get his attention. *But the Lord provided a great fish to swallow Jonah, and Jonah was inside the fish three days and three nights,* Jonah 1:17. God had given Jonah instructions to preach in the city of Nineveh, but Jonah didn't like those people and didn't want to go. He did, however, repent inside that great fish, and when the fish vomited him onto dry land, Jonah went and preached to Nineveh.

Be thoughtful of your pastor. You may think your church is the greatest congregation on earth. You may think your pastor is incredibly blessed because God gave him the privilege of serving your church. But to him, your church may be like Nineveh! Nobody wanted to go preach in Nineveh—God had to force Jonah to do it, and yet Jonah saw great results there because the citizens of Nineveh humbled themselves. Pastors are often accused of being arrogant, and some are. Most of the time, however, what seems like arrogance is merely a defensive posture against a haughty church. Humble people tend to produce humble leaders. A humble pastor can lead a proud church to humility, but only if he can survive long enough.

Prophets are often afraid of the consequences of being obedient to God. But, they fear more the consequences of disobedience. Consider

God's words in Jeremiah 1:17-19. *"Get yourself ready! Stand up and say to them whatever I command you. Do not be terrified by them, or I will terrify you before them. Today I have made you a fortified city, an iron pillar and a bronze wall to stand against the whole land—against the kings of Judah, its officials, its priests and the people of the land. They will fight against you but will not overcome you, for I am with you and will rescue you,"* declares the Lord. If you are a pastor, and you are willing to ask yourself, "Am I a hireling or a shepherd," then the answer may lie in how you answer this question: "Am I more terrified of my congregation or terrified of disobeying God?"

Church member, notice what God said to Jeremiah: *I will terrify you.* If your pastor is truly called to the ministry, then God has called him to be fearless of **you**. To stand up to **you**. To tell **you** things that **you** don't want to hear. Before you criticize his leadership, take a few moments and put yourself in his place before God.

True shepherds are leaders. They hear from God and deliver his messages. There is one other thing that separates the true shepherds from the false. You may have noticed Jeremiah's words, *Ah, Sovereign Lord.* Even in his reluctance, Jeremiah still recognized that God reigns in his life. You see a lot of God's true shepherds in the scripture refer to the sovereignty of God. When you understand that God is sovereign, you understand, as I shared in Part One, that God reigns over each of us, whether or not we like it or accept it. A false shepherd will not accept God's sovereignty in his life.

Peter addressed this issue in his second epistle, Chapter 2:1. *But there were also false prophets among the people, just as there will be false teachers among you. They will secretly introduce destructive heresies, even denying the sovereign Lord who bought them—bringing swift destruction on themselves.* Do you realize what Peter was saying? These false prophets and teachers don't necessarily preach that Jesus isn't the Savior. On the contrary, they often preach Jesus very well. But they deny that he is sovereign. In other words, they believe they can still do what they want, when they want, and how they want. Remember what God said to Jeremiah? *You must go to everyone I send you to and say whatever I command you.*

To paraphrase, God was saying that he was in charge, not Jeremiah. He is sovereign. I once served under a pastor who said to me on more than one occasion, "I know what the Bible says, but that's not how we're going to do it!" In fact, he got rather agitated with me whenever I reminded him of our biblical obligations. This pastor preached God's word, but didn't believe he had to live by it. He did not recognize that God is sovereign in his life. You may recall from Chapter 7 the words of Jesus, concerning the Pharisees, *"But do not do what they do, for they do not practice what they preach."* Matthew 23:3

While it is true that there are false shepherds in the church, according to God's Word, it is also true that most of God's pastors are trying their very best to be true to God's expectations. A true shepherd is a leader who learns from his mistakes, who encourages, educates, and expects positive results. He hears from God and delivers God's messages. He recognizes that God is sovereign, that he reigns over us, and he leads others to this truth. He seeks to bring the lost to true salvation, not fire insurance. He leads others to holiness through confession and repentance, because he himself lives that way. Shepherds teach us these truths and help guide us along the narrow path. This is the truth about shepherds.

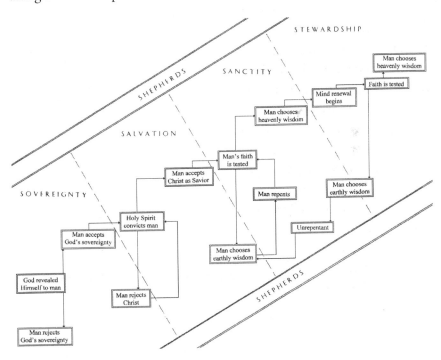

SHEPHERDS

How have these five truths impacted you? Are you a Christian? If not, why not? What would it take to convince you that you need salvation? My prayer is that through this book you have come to a greater understanding of just how much God loves you, and how much he has done to make salvation possible for you. Hopefully you recognize that history didn't just happen through a series of unrelated events, but was orchestrated by a loving Father who desires that you seek him. If God is convicting you about your eternal destiny, please, talk to him. Ask him to forgive your sinfulness and save you. Ask him to renew your mind and transform you into someone who resembles him. Set your mind on becoming a disciple!

If you are already saved, are you a disciple yet? Do you know that more has been changed in you than just the status of your soul? Is God renewing your mind, or have you not surrendered it to him yet? Do you feel loved by your Father, or do you feel disappointed? Do you find joy in waking up each morning, wondering what God will do with you today, or do you trudge through life, just getting through. God does not promise that life will be easy, and it is certainly not my intention to give that impression. I have been through painful experiences, some of which I have shared in this text. What I didn't share with you was the agony, the occasional despair, and the grieving. But let me share this: out of all of it, my God was there, and always a loving Father, even when I didn't feel loved. Through it all, he has made me stronger and drawn me closer to him. Being a disciple is not always easy, but it is rewarding beyond description. There is no One more deserving of your devotion than the One who made you. May God bless you on your journey.

PART FIVE REVIEW

Terms to Remember:
SHEPHERD—one who is called to lead God's local congregation
PROPHECY—the gift of communicating God's will to his people

Questions to think about:
HOW OFTEN DO YOU PRAY FOR YOUR PASTOR?

About the Author

John R. Gaters is the pastor of Pinson Baptist church in western Tennessee. His life experiences, preaching ministry, and service in the local church have ignited a passion for teaching the deep truths about God in a clear and easy-to-understand format. His call is to pass these truths on to his own congregation and as far beyond as God will allow. John is a former minister of music and education, and his wife, Angela, has also served in vocational children's ministry. They have three grown children.

Printed in the United States
By Bookmasters